All best wishes
to
Daniel

a. Louise Ztaman

Restoring Lost Times

Savannah's Anna Colquitt Hunter

Tiger Iron Press
Savannah, Georgia

Restoring Lost Times

By

A. Louise Staman

Tiger Iron Press

Front cover painting by Anna Colquitt Hunter, courtesy of the Telfair Museums
Back cover painting by Anna Colquitt Hunter

Book design by E. Michael Staman, Mike.Staman@TigerIronPress.com

Library of Congress Cataloging-in-Publication Data
Restoring Lost Times / A. Louise Staman
ISBN 978-0-9851745-9-0

Search by: Anna Colquitt Hunter, History of Savannah, Historic Preservation, Georgia History, Historic Savannah Foundation, History of SCAD, Women's History

First Edition: 2018

Printed in the United States of America

Dedication

In loving memory of F. F. Lofgren, my dad.

Attributions

Agnes Scott College, McCain Library, Marianne Bradley: who provided information on the teen years of Anna Colquitt Hunter.

Michael Ching, 2017 Savannah composer-in-residence for The Voice: for his encouragement, information, and wonderful opera, *Anna Hunter, The Spirit of Savannah.*

Colquitt descendants, particularly Anna's grandchildren, Dr. Harriet Ross Jardine in particular: who provided virtually all of the photos of Anna as well as photos of her art and copies of Anna's speeches.

Davenport House, Jamie Credle: for telephone interviews and much unpublished history on Anna Hunter and the founding of this house and the Historic Savannah Foundation.

Georgia Historical Society: providing books and significant archives.

Historic Savannah Foundation and Daniel Carey: provided information and pointing to significant directions regarding the pursuit of my subject.

Library of Congress: provided free access to Civil War photos and buildings in and around Savannah. General pictures without attribution not of Anna Colquitt or her art came from this source.

Savannah Municipal Archives; for general Savannah information.

Savannah Country Day School: for answers by telephone regarding Anna's early childhood education.

Savannah Live Oak Public Library, Bull Street Library: provided a huge file on Anna Hunter, early Savannah indexes, free access to Savannah newspapers via microfilm, and the unpublished biography of Anna Hunter, *Anna's Annals.*

Table of Contents

Chapter 1

Savannah's First Escape

Today, gazing at Savannah's stately and beautiful Historic District, it is hard to imagine that it could ever have been in danger of destruction. In fact, the District has stood in imminent danger of total ruin not once, but twice. Now this impressive area seems timeless, with live oaks draped in Spanish moss, huge magnolias, manicured gardens, flowers everywhere, and historic homes, buildings, and churches arranged in twenty-two lush squares. Two people, one man and one woman, of different temperaments and purpose and living in different eras, are responsible for the preservation of this scene, now visited by millions of people from all over the world. These two "saviors" could not be more different: General William Tecumseh Sherman and Anna Colquitt Hunter. All that General Sherman needed to destroy Savannah was to nod his head. All that Anna Hunter needed for the demolition of Savannah's Historic District was to turn her back.

Savannah's present Historic District is about the same size as the entire town was in 1864, when Sherman paid his visit. Its total population then was only about 20,000, 8,000 of whom were slaves. All of them knew the dreaded General was coming, as inexorably as death itself. They had already heard what he did to Atlanta on November 16. That night he burned

General William Tecumseh Sherman

almost the entire city. As William T. Sherman sat comfortably in Judge Lyon's expropriated Atlanta mansion, eating a simple supper, a military band played outside. Most of the windows of the home reflected orange and yellows. Atlanta was ablaze: towering flames shattered the sky, punctuated by explosions of shells stored within the city. As one witness put it: "Presently the skeletons of great warehouses stand out in relief against . . . sheets of roaring, blazing, furious flames . . . as one fire sinks, another rises . . . hard, angry, dreadful to look upon."

Later that night an Ohio officer of Sherman's Fourteenth Corps stated, "I saw Gen. Sherman walking about the streets of the blazing city paying no heed to the flames seemingly nothing." That officer concluded much the same about Sherman as others would later surmise: "I don't believe he has any mercy in his composition."

Following Atlanta's destruction, Sherman led his troops southeast. It is hard to imagine what the people of Savannah were thinking as they heard about Atlanta and the path that Sherman was taking, getting closer each day – looting, destroying, and burning all the way. As he approached Decatur, one woman reported, "As far as the eye could reach, the lurid flames of burning buildings lit up the heavens. I could stand out on the verandah and for two or three miles watch as they came on. I could mark when they reached the residence of each and every friend on the road."

On he went cutting a swath sixty miles wide with his troops – to Milledgeville, fighting, taking, burning and freeing those in prison there. Sherman was obsessed by the need to destroy everything the Confederates might need to continue the already protracted Civil War. He was desperate to end the struggle by any means possible. After Milledgeville's destruction, Sherman continued his march to the east – to Millen and Fort McAllister, then on to that beautiful town of Savannah on the eastern coast of Georgia. Many historical sources report that Sherman had every intention of destroying

Making "Sherman's Neckties"

Savannah with all of the vengeance he had shown to Atlanta. Two major events, however, caused him to change his initial course of action. On December 6, Sherman received orders from Ulysses S. Grant to lead his troops north to provide reinforcements for the assault on General Robert E. Lee's army in Virginia. These orders caused Sherman to halt his immediate plans to burn Savannah. After all, he had already surrounded the town with about 60,000 to 70,000 troops and cut off all food, supplies and reinforcements.

He could starve them out if he so desired. In addition, he had already halted any future railroad activity in the area by picking up the rails and throwing them into huge bonfires – then when they were white-hot, bending them around trees – making "Sherman's neckties," as they were called.

The second reason he didn't destroy Savannah is the result of the Confederate command of General Hardee (with the full knowledge and agreement of General Beauregard). On December 17, 1864, Sherman wrote a letter to Confederate General Hardee demanding the surrender of Savannah. Not unexpectedly, Hardee refused. As Sherman generally did before the destruction of a town, he then ordered the evacuation of all civilians. What he did not suspect at the time was that General Hardee then ordered that all Confederate troops also evacuate to South Carolina. Hardee had 10,000 to 15,000 troops, no reinforcements and dwindling supplies. Which would be better? To allow these troops to be slaughtered by Sherman's overwhelming force? Or to conserve these men to continue their fight in the future (perhaps in South Carolina) when the sides would be more equal? And so at daybreak on December 20, Confederate soldiers began their retreat from Savannah along with most of the civilians, crossing their temporary pontoon bridge into South Carolina. General Hardee never surrendered the city of Savannah to the Union Army – the Mayor of Savannah did, sending General Sherman the following note on December 21:

> *SIR: The city of Savannah was last night evacuated by the Confederate military and is now entirely defenseless. As chief magistrate of the city I respectfully request your protection of the lives and private property of the citizens and women and children.*
>
> *Trusting that this appeal to your generosity and humanity may favorably influence your action, I have the honor to be your obedient servant,*
>
> *R.D. Arnold, Mayor of Savannah*

Before their departure, the Confederates destroyed anything they believed might be of use to the Yankees, including that pontoon bridge. They even blew up their own ship *Savannah,* which lit up the sky with its flames.

The Confederates gave Sherman no reason to burn Savannah – all of the soldiers had already left the city. Defenseless old men, women, children, and slaves were all that were left, who gave weak smiles and little waves to the conquering Yankees as they entered the town. There was little for Sherman and his troops to do, except to take over the city – peacefully. On December 22, 1864 General W.T. Sherman presented the entire city of Savannah as a Christmas present to Abraham Lincoln – along with heavy artillery the Rebels had not been able to move and twenty-five thousand bales of cotton. Savannah was saved from destruction, not because of Sherman's mercy or compassion, not because the city was so beautiful, or because Sherman might have had a girlfriend who lived there, or because he was a Mason like many residents – as some have suggested – but because there was no one left to fight.

Chapter 2

Anna's Ancestors and Early Childhood

Twenty-eight years after Sherman's capture of Savannah, little Anna Colquitt was born on January 21, 1892, in Anniston, Alabama. It is clear from her own writings that she was not pleased to have been born outside of Savannah, where she spent most of her life. "My family has always lived in Savannah and they were just temporarily in Alabama; that trip was a mistake." A little research reveals that Anna's statement was more wishful thinking than fact. There was no business or vacation trip to Anniston at the time of her birth; Anna's family resided there.

However, Anna's genealogical records clearly show how deeply entrenched her family was in Savannah. Both sides of her family are of "noble" linage, full of statesmen, doctors, lawyers, and plantation owners. Anna's parents were Walter Wellborn Colquitt and Matilda (Lilla) Habersham Colquitt. The distinguished name, "Habersham, on her mother's side shows that Anna was a direct descendent of James Habersham, who worked with General Oglethorpe in the founding of the Colony of Georgia." The name "Colquitt" was equally prominent in significant historical records, including a U.S. senator and a governor of Georgia.

Anna's grandmother Josephine Clay Habersham lived with her husband, William Neyle Habersham in Savannah when Sherman paid that town his unwelcome visit. Her 1863 diary still exists and reveals stunning similarities between Josephine and her granddaughter Anna. Both were strong, sensitive, gregarious women, lovers of music, the arts, literature. Both loved to dance and sing, were accomplished musicians and enjoyed parties; they were in fact often the life of these fêtes. Josephine and Anna were also both fluent in French and often wrote or spoke in that language to intimates. Finally, both wrote well, dressed well, and observed the styles of the times.

Although Josephine died when Anna was only a baby, both would love and enjoy the stately Habersham summer home "Avon," (named after Shakespeare's Stratford on Avon) on the Vernon River, about ten miles south of Savannah – a place apart, catching the breeze (if there was one), with large lazy live oaks and fruit trees – a beautiful and peaceful respite. Both women were smart, beautiful, high strung and often influential. One stark difference between these two, however, is that Josephine was privileged and wealthy, while Anna was not.

Unfortunately, both women would also know great sorrow. Josephine Habersham's 1863 diary (not published until 1958, entitled *Ebb Tide: As Seen through the Diary of*

Josephine Clay Habersham) reveals in detail the profound influence the Civil War had upon her, her family and others. In its early pages Josephine expresses her desire to teach those Yankees a lesson and chase them from the South! But as the war drags on Josephine begins to realize the enormous power and wealth of the North. Two of her sons became Confederate soldiers who fought at the front in many major battles. The letters Josephine writes to them and (much more important for her) the letters she receives from her sons Joseph Clay and William Neyle, Jr. ("Willie") form the backbone of the diary.

Then suddenly the diary ends – practically in mid-sentence. There would be no more entries by Josephine, for her two sons were killed in the Battle of Atlanta on the same day and within the same hour. Later referring to their deaths, Josephine quoted the lines of Tennyson:

> I sometimes hold it half a sin
> To put in words the grief I feel

Both brothers are buried together in the Habersham plot in Savannah's Laurel Grove Cemetery. Their inscription reads, "And in their death they were not divided." Margaret Mitchell would immortalize these two brothers, modeling them for the fictional Tarleton twins in *Gone with the Wind.* As for Anna Colquitt Hunter's great despair, it forms a significant part of her adult life and will be discussed later.

Savannah's Union Station, C1904

<u>South Front</u>

**Savannah's
Cotton Exchange
at
100 East Bay St.**

Anna was the sixth of seven children of W. Wellborn and Lilla Colquitt: little Lilla (born in 1874), Hattie (1876), Neyle (1878), Mabelle (1879) and Joe (1881), followed by an eleven-year hiatus. Then in 1892 Anna was born, followed by Wellborn in 1895. Although the Colquitts sometimes did not have much money, they schooled their children in much the same way as the Habershams. Music, particularly the classics, was emphasized, both heard and played nearly every day. And "we were read Dickens and other classics by the hour." In Anna's childhood, she spent much of her time at Avon, the Habersham summer home where many of her well-schooled relatives lived. While she loved those times, she also enjoyed and sought out the hubbub of Savannah, which by the turn of the century was once again experiencing good times.

The huge Savannah Union Station, finished in 1902, linked this town by rail to the rest of the country. Anna could even take a train with passenger seats made of wicker and red velvet to the beach at nearby Tybee Island. Cotton again became king, (as it was before the Civil War) and was exported throughout the states and to other nations, along with resin and lumber. The cotton center was a stately building facing the Savannah River, built by the nationally acclaimed Boston architect William G. Preston. Known as the Savannah Cotton Exchange, the people in this building, along with those in a similar structure in Liverpool, England, set international cotton prices.

The black community also grew stronger, both culturally and economically, in spite of continued prejudice.

The older historic district that Sherman had saved from obliteration once again became gentrified and polished. Ancient buildings within that area reflected this prosperity. They were cherished and kept up. Examples include: The Pirate's House (1754); the Olde Pink House (1771) – built by James Habersham Jr.; and the Juliette Gordon Low House (1821), who founded the Girl Scouts. In addition, the 1812 Telfair mansion would become one of the most significant museums in the South: The Telfair Academy of Arts and Sciences. Many of the local places of worship also enjoyed turn-of-the-century care and restoration. They include: The Lutheran Church of the Ascension, The Independent Presbyterian Church, St. John the Baptist Catholic Church; First African Baptist Church, and Temple Mickve Israel.

Anna interacted with her many brothers and sisters in spite of the fact that most of them were much older. Apparently, her parents were not strict or firm disciplinarians. "Our parents never seemed to mind what we did, and though it was a decade or more before children were allowed to express themselves, we did, as we were free agents." Anna loved and often emulated her older siblings, particularly her sister Hattie (sixteen years older than she). Family gatherings generally consisted of "…much talk and hilarity, laughter and teasing." Although all of the Colquitt children were considered handsome and healthy, many agreed that Lilla and Anna were "more than just pretty."

Olde Pink House

Formerly the Habersham House

c. 1940

Pirates' House on Broad Street

c. 1940

Exactly when Anna Colquitt started formal schooling is not clear. Compulsory school attendance was not enacted by the state of Georgia until 1916, when Anna was twenty-four. The Minimum Foundation Program of 1949 was the first to establish a uniform school term of nine months. Even when free public education was available, it was not uncommon for parents (particularly farmers) to take their children out of school to help with the planting, the harvest and other chores. In wealthy families boys were often sent to military schools, while girls were sometimes given no formal training at all beyond the 3 R's. Wealthier girls were often sent to finishing school where writing, speech, posture, poise, and other important rules of etiquette were taught to young ladies soon to be married. The acronym LORD could be used to describe the goal of the finishing school: Loyalty, Obedience, Respect, and Duty.

Elementary schools in the United States before and after 1900 generally used strict, sometimes harsh discipline. Corporal punishment was common. Teaching by rote and memorization with students having little or no freedom for creative thought or discussion was the norm. Anna had the advantage of her mother's musical instruction, reading of the classics, and elementary French in the home. She also attended elementary school, known for its large classes and lessons by rote. There is no evidence that Anna's strong personality was in any way thwarted by elementary school teachers or regulations. In a note to her sister, Anna wrote, "I forgot to tell you . . . that I wrote my name Anna Columbus in school."

By the time Anna was older, a gentle, highly-educated woman had begun to address the subject of the schooling of girls in Savannah. She would not only change the course of Anna's education, but also that of countless others: Nina Anderson Pape. She was born in Savannah to a prominent, traditional family. Her grandfather Edward Clifford Anderson had been mayor of Savannah for seven years. Miss Pape, as she was known, was raised in the traditional, conservative manner so common to upper-class Savannah ladies at the turn of the century. She was tutored at Savannah's Girls High School and then (like many other upper-class young Georgian women) attended a finishing school: Madame LeFèbvre's French Finishing School in Baltimore.

To all appearances Miss Pape seemed the personification of traditional Southern values. She dressed in a more nineteenth-century manner than the "modern style" after the turn of the century: long dark dresses, high collars, perhaps a modest string of pearls, and hair piled high in a bun. Here was a native upper-class Savannahian with all the proper credentials to be a true conservative Victorian schoolmistress: a soft-spoken, lovely, polite and always proper Southern Belle . . . with one exception: her rebellious mind.

She did not consider her education finished by a finishing school, no matter how famous. She continued her schooling with correspondence courses at the University of Chicago and also attended classes at the Teachers College of Columbia University. There she encountered the ideas of German educator and philosopher Frederic Froebel, who eschewed the notions of memorization and rote learning in a "spare the rod and spoil the child" atmosphere for elementary school. Instead, he proposed the concept of kindergartens where play and creative interaction were encouraged. Toys in the form of different shapes and sizes were freely given out, and nature became a significant topic for discussion. First-hand experience was the goal of frequent field trips. According to Froebel, even the youngest child should be treated as an important and unique individual. Although strict discipline was fine, it should be used in an atmosphere of love and understanding.

Miss Pape took Froebel's ideas with her when she returned to Savannah. The more she learned, the more she came to realize that the female mind was too often neglected. Why not give females an academic education as rigorous as the males – or at least the same educational opportunity? Miss Pape decided to do something about the education of Savannah's girls and women. However, she was not just thinking of improving women's brainpower. She had an additional goal: teaching girls the concept of giving back to their community. In this realm she taught by example. She created the Froebel Society in Savannah, a King's Daughters chapter, which served to disseminate Froebel's educational philosophy. The Froebel Society was also responsible for the establishment of the Fresh-Air Home, providing underprivileged children with trips to the ocean and beaches of nearby Tybee Island. She helped to create seven kindergartens in poor neighborhoods throughout the city, not unlike the

"Head Start Programs" decades later. Before Nina Anderson Pape, there was no real kindergarten in Savannah. She helped to establish playgrounds, particularly in poorer neighborhoods, so that children could have a place of their own to play.

Her crowning achievement came in about 1905 when she founded the Pape School, a private educational facility for upper-class girls, which eventually ranged from kindergarten through grade twelve. Students at this school were given small classes, individual attention and rigorous academics, in addition to physical education and frequent nature studies and field trips. Essentially, Miss Pape replaced the ideals of the finishing school (Loyalty, Obedience, Respect and Duty) with new ones: Character, Leadership, Service, and Scholarship. Anna Colquitt was one of the first students in Pape's "Upper School" (high school).

Miss Pape found accomplished and educated teachers for her little school in a small town of the Deep South. The faculty at Pape held diplomas from Emory, Johns Hopkins, Columbia, Swarthmore, Vassar, Minnesota, and Vanderbilt, not counting the French teachers for the lower and upper schools. One held the *Brevet supérieur du Convent de Notre Dame du Calvaire, à Besons près Paris,* Columbia University. The other held the *Brevet supérieur,* Bon Rivage, Switzerland. The Pape philosophy paid off handsomely. Of the 116 young women who received diplomas from Pape between 1915 and 1934, seventy-seven went on to a four-year college (many were the finest in the nation), three to junior college and five went on to finishing school. Sixty-six percent of these graduates went to college, most of them out-of-state, primarily in the Northeast. The most popular of these northern schools for Pape graduates was Smith, followed by Randolph-Macon and Wellesley. Of the girls who attended the public Savannah High School during the same time period, almost none went on to college. And nearly all of those who went chose a teachers' college or a secretarial school.

Since Anna's family was nearly always short of money, one must wonder how her parents scraped up the funds to give her such a fine education. The answer lies in the Pape School philosophy. Nina Pape founded a private school exclusively for young girls who came from "good families," whether they had the wherewithal to pay for it or not. Because of her background and family standing, Anna could attend the Pape School at greatly reduced prices or even for free. She was not the only student to receive financial support in order to attend. Miss Pape even took some of her students temporarily into her own home when a tragedy or crisis occurred within their family.

Anna Colquitt, 1912
(Courtesy of Agnes Scott College)

When it came to community service, Nina Pape herself led by example, not just with the kindergarten and fresh-air projects for disadvantaged children and the establishment of the Pape School, but also with essential services to her distant cousin Juliette Gordon Low in helping to found the Girl Scouts and allowing the Pape School to serve as the first training ground for young Scouts.

Miss Pape entered every class at her school and greeted all of her students with, "Good Morning, children!" The response was always the same: "The same to you, Miss Pape!" Although she was gentle and kind, many students feared her. She was tall, angular, aristocratic, always correct in posture and actions, with a deeply observant stare.

As one student put it, "She had a somewhat cavernous voice . . . and a way of emphasizing a point by wagging her middle and index fingers at her listener; it did sort of rivet your attention." The Pape School continued for eleven years following the death of Nina A. Pape in 1944. Then in 1955 its buildings were purchased by the New Country Day School, which also adopted much of Miss Pape's philosophy, along with many of the school's remaining teachers and students. This school, soon renamed the Savannah Country Day School, remains to this day one of the finest college preparatory schools not just in Georgia, but in the nation.

Anna "mugging" for the camera, c. 1905

In June, 1906, when Anna was only fourteen, her mother died at age fifty-three. Apparently, she also had mental illness at the time. This death would not affect Anna's older siblings as much as the younger two children. After all, the next oldest offspring would have been twenty-four. The youngest, Wellborn, was ten. If Anna wrote down her reaction to this death, it has not survived. Perhaps her feelings were similar to her grandmother Josephine's upon the death of her two sons – too difficult for words.

In 1910 Anna was admitted to Agnes Scott College (located in Decatur, GA) as an irregular student, meaning that she did not intend to follow the course work leading to a particular degree. It was founded in 1889 by Presbyterian Minister Frank H. Gaines as a private liberal arts college for women, and named after the mother of its most significant benefactor, George Washington Scott.

As an irregular student at Agnes Scott, Anna was free to pick and choose the many courses and activities afforded by this school. She chose to enter the School of Music, Art and Expression. She had a beautiful voice and sang first soprano in the glee club. She always loved dramatics and participated in many dramatic activities, including playing roles in Shakespeare's *As You Like It*, and *A Mid-Summer Night's Dream*. As for expression, clearly she excelled in writing, becoming Class Poet in 1912 and winning the college's "English Prize" for that year. She was also an associate editor of the school yearbook, *Silhouette*. There is no record that she ever took one of the school's art classes. This form of expression did not become important to her until she was a much older woman.

Anna also excelled in sports at her school. She belonged to the Tennis Club, played first base on the baseball team, and was a forward on the basketball team. Yet she also had time for many school clubs: The Bull Dog Club, The Week-End Club, Corridor Lieutenant for the RSH Fire Department and the South Georgia Club.

Anna's College Activities

(Images courtesy of Agnes Scott 1911 and 1912 yearbook, *Silhouette*)

From Upper Left:
Baseball Team
Glee Club
Sophomore Basketball Team
R. S. H. Fire Department
Bull Dog Club
Inman hall Fire Brigade
Silhouette Staff
South Georgia Club

Chapter 3

Marriage

In addition to all of her Agnes Scott activities, Anna Colquitt found a beau: George Lewis Cope Hunter, one year older than she, who was then a student at the University of Georgia. By all accounts, they fell deeply in love. They both dropped out of college and were married in Savannah on October 22, 1913.

Less than two months after the wedding Anna's father, W. Wellborn Colquitt, died unexpectedly. The sudden losses of Anna's parents may have triggered a feeling of possessiveness within her regarding her new husband. She easily became jealous of any woman George looked at, often causing turbulence within the marriage. Exacerbating the situation was the nearly-always lack of money within the family household.

Anna's daughter Harriot Hunter Jardine commented on this situation in her book *Anna's Annals*:

"Another significant factor in their misunderstandings was the fact that early in their marriage it was necessary to live in the family home on 31st Street with George's widowed mother and her daughter Julia, Julia's husband, Robert (Bob) Aldrich and their three children." Apparently, Anna and her mother-in-law ("Nanny") were continually at odds. This was understandable because George was the apple of his mother's eye and she never thought too highly of the woman her son married although there was no open hostility, at least not in front of the children . . . . Julia, George's older sister, was also jealous of Anna (and vice versa); she [Anna] was a stunningly beautiful woman and remained so into her nineties. Both had beautiful voices, and their rivalry in the Christ Church choir was well known.

Jardine then gives an example of the hostility between Anna and her mother-in-law. "Nanny" gave Anna a present: a beautiful expensive gold mesh coin purse with a gold clasp and a little ruby, diamond and pearl on each side. "In her usual slapdash fashion, Anna set it down on the counter in the local McCrory's and a passerby apparently picked it up." Jardine continues, "Nanny never tired of reminding Anna how careless she had been. Her remonstrations went on for years. [S]he never let her forget it."

Anna and George had three children: Harriot (born in 1915), George, Jr. (born in 1918), and Nancy (born in 1919). In spite of their financial situation, Anna, like nearly every

Right: Anna with baby George

Below: Anna with Harriot and George

other Southern family above sheer poverty, had a cook and a nurse/nanny of sorts. Rose the cook did not allow anyone in "her" kitchen. She dominated everywhere she could. "She was short, black, and jolly in spite of her imperious ways and she loved the family dearly."

Laura, who took care of the children, was "a sour faced black woman who these days could easily be brought to court on charges of child abuse." Jardine did not believe that her mother knew about the abuses of this "tall ungainly woman who sailed around the house in black and would occasionally lock a child in the closet for misbehavior and who seemed to be obsessed with 'ghosts,' 'ha'nts' and threatening fantasies."

Anna's three children disliked and feared Laura. They never knew when one of her fantasies would strike. For example, Harriot remembered that when she was seven, she relaxed in a chair and put her hands up behind her head. Laura looked at the child and announced that her position in the chair meant that she hated her mother.

Anna's husband George never seemed to be able to get a job and hold it for long. At one point he had to declare bankruptcy, which in those days was viewed as not just a reversal of fortune, but also a disgrace. Thanks to his father's connections, he got a job at the Savannah Bank & Trust, then became a salesman for a fertilizer company, later became a certified public accountant and worked for the company of Neville, McIver & Barnes. George's unsteady job history sometimes required his family to move. Because of their financial difficulties, they were not able to buy a house –

always renting, a fact that hurt their social status within the community. To help defray costs, Anna started working early in her marriage. Because her older siblings Hattie and Nyle worked for the *Savannah Evening Press,* Anna was able to get a job there, beginning what would become a long and successful newspaper career. But her pay in those early days was paltry.

In spite of their precarious financial status, George and Anna did manage to attain and maintain a good social standing within the community. Both were members of a closely knit, socially prominent group called "The E.B.'s," a somewhat secret society. Even the initials were held in secrecy. George was also a Mason and a member of the National Guard. Both loved music. Anna played the piano and harbored a personal desire to become an opera star. George had a fine tenor voice and played the guitar. Anna also excelled at acting. She gained prominence in Savannah's Little Theater as well as the church choir.

Anna as "Sequoia" [sic], 1933

They made a striking couple. Both were handsome, interesting, and in love. Their daughter Harriot Jardine noted the differences between her parents: "Anna was outspoken, volatile, humorous and very much oriented to the cultural life of the day . . . . George on the other hand, was quiet, retiring, and unassuming although fun-loving; he was very handsome and had a shy sense of humor." But in spite of their differences, they were obviously madly in love. Anna's daughter Harriot says, "Among my own memories: Many times we three kids were in the car waiting to be taken for a Sunday drive while Mother and Daddy were standing in the hallway, oblivious to all, hugging and kissing."

Harriot continues:

> Mother had a beautiful old chest, probably her original "Hope Chest," with a pink brocade top, studded with gold braids. One afternoon in my teens my curiosity overcame me and I opened the chest to discover many old letters. I read with increasing amazement and romantic delight the love letters exchanged by my parents at various times; one particular memorable series was the exchange in which Mother accused Daddy of a flirtation which he vigorously denied in letter after letter, protesting his undying devotion and everlasting fidelity in almost poetical terms. I believe my mother burned these letters before she left for Africa [during World War II] in case something should happen to her.

At a time when the Hunters were scrambling for money, the city of Savannah itself began to fall on hard times. Its seaport started losing customers as the state's production of cotton declined. It is hard to believe that a tiny bug could cause so much damage to a state's or a city's economy. Certainly Savannah's leaders in the 1920s did not foresee that such a seemingly insignificant bug, the boll weevil, could derail the economics of such a large seaport. But that is what happened. No one in power at that time foresaw the need to diversify exports. After all, cotton had been King for decades. Why should anyone worry about cotton? But that small bug changed everything.

The invasion of the boll weevil began when it crossed the border from Mexico into Texas in about 1894. This insect with a long nose and voracious appetite laid its eggs in the tiny leaves surrounding the cotton blossom, thus preventing the boll where the cotton developed from growing. At first, no one paid any attention to that insidious insect. However, by 1913 it had munched its way through almost all of the cotton crops in southwest Georgia and was headed toward the rest of the state with as much determination as Sherman himself. Farmers watched helplessly as field after field of cotton was destroyed. Nothing could stop it.

Cotton was measured in 500-pound bales. In 1879 Georgia produced 2,794,295 bales of cotton, second only to Texas in cotton production. With the boll weevil epidemic, that production declined steadily nearly every year. By 1923 Georgia produced only 588,000 bales of cotton, with no end of decline in sight. No one in Savannah had imagined such a loss in cotton exports, let alone tried to diversify. The loss to Savannah and its seaport was staggering.

Then came the stock market crash of 1929, causing a major and lengthy depression not just within Georgia, but everywhere in the United States, and even worldwide. During these difficult years the unemployment rate soared, making it even harder for George to get employment. The family moved to Florida where George took temporary jobs. They lived in several different rentals in the early 1930s. However, George was an excellent accountant. In 1933 he took federal tests for employment and got one of the highest scores in the nation. As a result he went to Washington to work as a Federal Land Bank examiner under Franklin D. Roosevelt at $3300 per year, a good salary (equaling $59,583 in 2016) in those times. Finally, he had the job that he wanted.

But it was not to be. In March, 1936 George Hunter died suddenly of a gastric hemorrhage at the age of forty-four. Anna "found herself faced with the loss of her lover of 23 years, the support and education of three children and no home to go to." Anna and her children accompanied George's body from Washington to Savannah for the funeral and burial. With his body in the train's freight car, the rest of his family squeezed together in a small stateroom. "Throughout the night Anna's body shook the Pullman berth with continuous dry sobs." In Savannah, they first spent time at Mrs. Gordon's Boarding House. The funeral took place at the home of George's mother on 31st Street.

A year or two before George's death, Anna's sister Hattie had purchased a pleasant small home called "The Card House" in the backwater village of Bluffton, SC, not far from Savannah.

Following George's death, Hattie invited Anna and her children to use this home. They accepted and spent several months there. Nancy and George went to high school in Bluffton. Anna had already made it clear to her daughter

Harriot that she would go back to college. When the family was packing following George's death, Anna handed Harriot some bars of soap.

"Here, you can take these back to college."

"Oh, Mom, am I going back to school?"

"Of course," Anna responded. "Don't be silly."

Card House in Bluffton, painting by A. Hunter

Hattie helped Anna and her children financially and provided a home for them, thereby giving Anna a chance to recover from her grief and begin to think about the future. What was she going to do to provide support for her children and herself? At that time (1936) the general motto of the nation regarding women and careers was "Woman's place is in the home!" What home? Hattie's? Anna had no home to retreat to – no assets, no prospects, and no real experience, except for her little job at the local newspaper. In the Card House Anna certainly had a lot to think about.

But at least with Hattie's moral and financial support, Anna had some time to grieve . . . and to ponder her future. When her granddaughter complained that her lettuce tasted bad, Anna told her that she had watered the plants with her tears, causing their biting taste. She also complained "'that a sad little bird with a mournful call was driving me crazy.'" The "sad song" turned out to be the mating call of the Carolina Chickadee. But with the peace and quiet of her little home and Hattie's support, Anna had a place to recover. "Later during Hattie's last years, Anna repaid her by going back to Bluffton to take care of her." After a few months in Bluffton, Anna felt strong enough to stand on her own two feet once again. She moved back to Savannah, rented a small place on Jones Street and reclaimed her old job on the *Savannah Evening Press*. She also worked some for the *Savannah Morning News*. In both cases she became a regular reporter. "I covered every beat but the courthouse. I loved that work." She wrote about fires, murders, city council meetings, and anything else she came across. In spite of her meager pay, she soon was noticed as an excellent reporter. She interviewed a Chicago editorialist visiting Savannah. He later wrote of her that "'[T]here is a newspaperwoman in Savannah who knows what she is doing …. I don't know what her salary is but whatever it is, they ought to double it.'" Anna's pay didn't double, but she got more and better assignments. She was "thrilled" when she was assigned to interview Franklin D. Roosevelt upon his Savannah visit. The newspaper also asked her to organize the society pages. During that reorganization she started the soon-to-be popular column, "Nobody's Business."

Slowly Anna's indomitable sense of humor returned. She even enjoyed laughing when the joke was at her expense. As an example:

During the Spanish Civil War, Franco was in the news almost every day. One day when her daughter was home for a visit, the name of Franco came up at the dinner table conversation. Everyone at the table was simply astonished at this newspaper woman who presumably kept up with everything, asking, "Who is Franco?" She joined in the burst of laughter when it was explained to her who Franco was. For years after that, if anyone in the family asked a stupid question, the rejoinder would invariably be: "Who is Franco?"

Chapter 4

The Threat of War

Although her newspaper assignments were mostly local, Anna took serious notice of the international scene and shuddered at what she feared might come. Most of the nation in the 1930s were isolationist, wanting to be left alone and also desperate to make a living during the harsh depression times. Still, the bombastic speeches of the little German despot with the toothbrush moustache troubled Anna. She could not ignore the gathering storm clouds that were becoming more and more ominous over Europe. She wondered if the United States could or should continue its isolationist ways.

The bombing of Pearl Harbor, which led directly to the entry of the United States into World War II, occurred on December 7, 1941. But it was not until 1942 that the United States really became involved in the War.

Anna Colquitt Hunter was fifty years old in 1942, a middle-aged (old?) widow with little or no money living in a small town in southern Georgia. She had only local newspaper and child-care experience. She had never lived or even traveled much outside the South. And her hometown Savannah was hardly more than a sleepy, provincial town, more rooted in the South's past glory days than in the future. Even Savannah's seaport activities were greatly curtailed. Like just about everything else in Savannah, the seaport was stale and relatively stagnant because of lower cotton exports. The elegant homes and plantations of former days were crumbling. The town itself was shrinking. What prospects did Anna, or Savannah for that matter, have?

Less than one month (November 13th, 1941) before Pearl Harbor, Anna's mother-in-law Harriot C. Hunter (known to the family as Nanny) died. The hard feelings between Nanny and Anna that began at the inception of Anna's marriage to George continued up to the time of Nanny's death. Instead of leaving anything to Anna, Nanny skipped over Anna – leaving her nothing – and gave her three children instead a nice portion of her inheritance. However, Anna's children did not agree with Nanny's decision to omit Anna from the will. And they did something about it.

Shortly before the New Year, Anna received a significant sum of money with a letter. The first sentence read, "Be it hereby foresworn that we, the undersigned, being of age and being lately come into an inheritance, do promise to give you in equal parts, that sum which will cover all bills, all debts incurred and all financial obligations as of January 1st, 1942 . . . . ." At the end of the letter they announce that they are not trying to pay her back for what she has given them, but rather ". . . because of the things you are."

Because of you, we have lived in this world, and seen the beauty of a tree, the glory of a sunset, the wonder of a flower;

Because of you, we have known what love was; and let that love instead of rule or principle be to us our guiding star;

Because of you, we have known music, and the sound of your voice echoing through the years from our childhood twilights;

Because of you, we knew and loved a great and simple man, and knew his faith in each of us and everything we were and did;

Because of you, we five are now one, and go on – with increasing courage and faith in our tradition.

Signed:
Harriot, age 27
George, age 25
Nancy, age 23

America's entry into the War changed everything – at least for Savannah. That practically useless old port quickly took on a new sheen. Tactical uses, war distribution – and ships – the need for new warships suddenly turned the metaphorical old "sow's ear" into a "silk purse" bulging with money. Due to her limited funds, Anna rented a small apartment near the Savannah River. Fourteen East Bay Street was cheap, and centrally located. In Anna's writings of the time she makes it clear that she did not want to be a wallflower in the War. She avidly read about events in Europe and elsewhere. She discussed the particulars of the War with others. Both she and her sister Harriot feared a long war that would "soon lose its luster."

In the first of her two war journals, Anna gives us the picture of a greatly-changed Savannah waterfront, which she could see from her apartment window. Usually an ideal place for long, leisurely strolls, parts of the waterfront suddenly became restricted. One needed a special pass even to take a walk. Ubiquitous patrols and armed soldiers interrupted the flaneur's reverie with questions and requests for identification papers. The once moribund port took on new life – lights night and day, the screaming of machines, clanging steel, men yelling, flying sparks. Huge cranes moved up and down – in giant monster work. Faster, hurry, the work went on – until finally the smashing of a bottle, champagne everywhere, followed by the huge whish into the water to the accompaniment of *The Star Spangled Banner,* and another ship was launched. One of Anna's newspaper assignments was to report on these launchings. She once said, "[I'll never] smell champagne again [without hearing] *The Star Spangled Banner* in my mind."

Because the government declared that attending a ship launching was pleasure driving, not business, gas was severely rationed. Anna and many others attended these events on bicycles. She even covered the launching of the first ship built in the U.S. for the British, the USS Gazelle. However, the fact that the ship was built for Great Britain was secret at the time.

Anna was surprised by the town's new appearance. "Savannah so changed. Ship building people etc. making big

Launch of a Liberty Ship, 1941

From the Library of Congress: "Less than five months from keel laying to launching ceremony was the record set by the Patrick Henry. This time is being reduced to 60 days in the construction of her sister ships of the "Liberty Ship" design. This standard design was selected by the Maritime Commission to meet the need for ships that can be built in existing yards in minimum time with the additional purpose of conserving materials vitally needed for the war production effort. Prefabrication of sections in special plants, replacing of riveting wherever possible by welding and other new departures all contribute to the speed of construction and saving of material and dead weight in these ships which are already proving their worth in the war on the Axis." 2,710 Liberty Ships were constructed between 1941 and 1945.

wages and spending like water. Shops crowded. Not a place in town for rent." Along the streets she saw, "People selling war bonds giving speeches – situation grim." She also scrutinized some shady dealings: "Have been shocked lately by various aspects of shipbuilding – lots of graft and big money being made . . . . Shocking allegations . . . . It's shameful to think that money is back of it and all involved."

Anna was in the war effort right from the start. Only eight days following the bombing of Pearl Harbor she wrote, "Susie Waring and I are going to start in an observation post next week as WAACs are going to take over Filter Center soon and we want to keep up work." Anna volunteered to be a plane spotter and also offered to spot and report passing ships. "Looked out over balcony this aft, and there were 9 sub-chasers. British! Don't know what it's all about but saw in paper French *S. S. Richelieu* in an American port. Wonder if they could have convoyed her to Charleston or somewhere." Two months later she gave this report: "This afternoon there were 24 little flat boats in the river. I was told they are landing barges. Tonight they are nestled so snugly in the peaceful river. It tears the heart out to think they will be used in such hideous missions." On her first official day as a plane spotter, she saw "Ruby 4 – out on old Buckhalter Road." Often the planes came in little groups, usually in twos or threes. But on January 14th 1943 she wrote in her journal, "Planes flying in 5's and 6's & one call of 18. Swarms of planes." She wondered if she would ever be able to identify an enemy plane merely by its sound.

She also volunteered to help a church redecorate and furnish a day room in a hospital for soldiers. Along with her jobs as plane and ship spotter, newspaper reporter, eyewitness to ship launchings, and hospital day room decorator, she also wrote what she referred to as "maudlin *in memoriam* verses" for $50.00 per hundred. Although she wasn't particularly proud of her verses, she was glad for the money.

Several of her journal entries mentioned gas and food rationing. In her December 20th, 1942 entry, she stated that gas rationing was so severe, she could not go to nearby Bluffton for Christmas with her family. And due to the gas problem she threw a New Year's Eve party at her Bay Street apartment, centrally located for her friends. She had little trouble with food rationing since she ate lunch nearly every day at the Pink House. Throughout all of the changes and minor difficulties of wartime Savannah, Anna had little patience for hoarders or those who complained. "The rich are griping a little about deprivations. No one is willing to suffer. The war is too far away."

She did everything she could think of to get closer to the war. She wanted to join the WAACs. Then she considered joining the WAVES. But as she said, "They are recruiting here. Boys." She then tried the Red Cross a second time, to no avail. "I have been turned down by the Red Cross again. Had wonderful letters. Must be age tho they don't say so. It is a bitter disappointment – foreign service. I had hoped to do reconstruction work later." Although she cited her rejections regarding her applications for service in the war, she didn't explain how she was finally accepted. Her sister Harriet shed light on that subject in her unpublished work *Anna's Annals*. ". . . [S]he conned a general she knew into persuading the Red Cross to take her as a field director at the age of 51." Even at an early age Anna was great at persuasion.

Chapter 5

The Red Cross

Thrilled, Anna began her wartime experience by going to Washington D. C. on the Fourth of July, 1943. There she began her Red Cross training for work overseas. "I was put in a room here with 4 girls. We are in a dormitory of American University. It is absurd for me to be in a dormitory . . . but I'm getting a big kick out of it. And it is exactly like being in the Army." However, she did not yet have her Red Cross assignment – and so began the waiting game. Along with other Red Cross recruits, she visited hospitals filled with wounded servicemen. "It is hard to see them, especially the mental patients – so young." One month later Anna was still in Washington – waiting to be assigned. "Well it is still interesting. The types here are amazing. Some splendid and friends I've made are swell and redeem faith in human nature." Yet she found the waiting difficult. She was impatient, eager for the delays and reclassifications to be over. "After some time of loafing [with] . . . no assignments some of

Anna Hunter Red Cross Photograph, 1943-1944

the girls volunteered to work in offices. I finally offered to work in infirmary here for trainees. I really enjoyed it. I have a new patient named Woodruff from Boston – most attractive. Funny thing happened. He asked me to buy a pair of pajamas. I went to clerk. [She] asked me what size. 'D' I said.

"Is he tall?' asked the girl.

"'I don't know,' I said. 'I've never seen him out of bed.'

"That joke sure went the rounds. Well I stayed in the infirmary about 10 days. Woodruff gave me a rush when he got out and we got quite serious but when he found out I was not out for what he was – he dropped me. I hope I meet him some time and can step on Him!"

In September, 1943 Anna was still waiting . . . essentially with nothing to do. On October 1st a maid came into Anna's dormitory room and asked her:

"Is you permanent?"

Anna replied, "I believe I is."

However, the very next day she wrote:

"Well, I got it pretty straight. Today we are going to New York. So excited. Can't believe it. Doesn't mean we'll clear but we're headed toward that goal. I've really become so attached to A.U. [American University] I feel like a graduate leaving his *Alma Mater.* But do I want to go!!"

She reflected on the beauty of her hometown in Georgia and on the magnificence of Washington, D. C. But she just wasn't built to sit back and enjoy beautiful views and security. She wanted to get out and do something. "There are still worlds to conquer." She spent most of the day of October 4th packing and saying good-bye to her friends. And then, "Can't believe it!" That was the last journal entry of October 4th, 1943.

The first line of October 5th had only two words: "New York!"

Then she continued, "Here at last! This means we are ready to go when the army calls. It is too wonderful. Came on special car on B & O . . . . When we crossed on ferry it was thrilling to see the N.Y. skyline. We are at Manhattan Towers 22 E. 38th . . . Have 15th floor. Single rooms bath telephone and very nice . . . We start training tomorrow."

Her training in New York was not rigorous. She had time to see the sights and visit friends. She saw the Rockefeller Center, Shrafts, Queens, and had "the best Chinese food ever" in Chinatown. She even went on a beagle hunt and "saw more rabbits than the hounds did." At first she was assigned to the Pepsi Cola Service Center. "It is really fun. Jerking soda and talking to the boys. Some are cocky and some so shy and sweet." She met Scottish soldiers "in full regalia" and tried out her French on two Frenchmen. She described her days as long, full of activity, parties, dinners, sight-seeing, serving soldiers, but at the end of nearly every day, she said, "I feel dead." She took men bowling twice a week, often took soldiers to the barber (working hard to keep them out of the bars), and played tennis with them. Nearly always one could find her talking with "the boys." Some returning soldiers were "sad, one getting divorced, one was torpedoed 5 times and lost his best friend." She remembered one soldier in particular: "He said he'd seen men go crazy before his eyes." In her war days in Savannah, she had wished she could invite soldiers into her apartment for some food and talk. However, she feared such invitations could lead to more than she bargained for. How could you separate the nice from the not so nice? And even in New York she was careful not to put herself in compromising positions. She enjoyed talking with nearly all of them within the relative safety of places like the Pepsi Cola Service Center. As one young man said, she had "poisonality." She met one patient who did nothing but stare out the window. She got him to walk and talk. While she was with him, a ping-pong table fell to the floor: he screamed.

She had great fun with a French soldier named Pascal, who spoke no English, He "has attached himself to me" . . . "Pascal helps me make cocoa at night & there is much *comme si comme ça* – and wild gesticulations in the kitchen. He is going to take me to a French restaurant in N.Y." In spite of her age, she was pretty, energetic, and had no trouble getting men to work together to accomplish what she wanted, which impressed her superiors.

Finally after many interviews and more periods of waiting, she received her classification. She was reclassified as an Assistant Club Director for rest homes for soldiers at a salary of $225 per month "plus maintenance." "It's a wonderful job," said Anna. "That part is swell but nobody seems to know when we will go."

Chapter 6

Anna in Africa

She soon found out. On November 28, 1943, Anna arrived in Casa Blanca. "It was thrilling getting our first glimpse of city. We had to go below tho to our cabins with port holes closed as we docked. Sound speaker called out units to disembark; we drove out in open trucks & saw first Arabs. The countryside is beautiful. Just like Biblical pictures."

Yet she still did not know her final destination. They spent their first night in Africa at a place called Camp Marshall, which she concluded must be on the way. On the way to where? There they stayed in barracks and slept on straw mattresses. For the first time, Anna ate in a mess hall, with mess kits, which the diners later scalded and washed in "big cauldrons over open fire." She noted that there were Italian prisoners working in the camp. Anna would spend four nights at this camp, so near the Mediterranean that she could see the water from the camp. At this juncture Anna concluded, "Africa smells! But scenery is beautiful." Always looking for something to do, Anna helped work on newspapers for the

Courrier. On December 2, Anna found out where she was going to be assigned. "I will go to Oran. I did not get a rest home in Italy – was disappointed but after all being on the Mediterranean should be nice. Seems there's a club there at Replacement Center where they need a new club director. They asked if I could rough it, so seems grim. But I want to go where someone is needed so hope this is chance to prove what I can do."

Anna took the train to Oran seven days later. She wished that she could help the Arabs and their children, who begged for candy and cigarettes at every stop. She arrived in Oran the following day and was stunned. She had been told stories of how ugly and awful Oran was and was delighted to discover the opposite. The city was beautiful, interesting, exotic, with

Solders Giving Their Milk to the Children of Oran

tall narrow buildings (often ancient), elaborate balconies and tiny winding streets. Oran was most certainly multicultural, with camels, jeeps, carts, a flock of sheep, people (black, brown, white and all shades in between) resplendent with color, set beside the sparkling blue sea.

During the war Hunter became fascinated by the Architecture of Oran.

Anna's response to her new environment was typical of so many of her previous responses on this adventure: "I am thrilled."

Anna's assignment in Oran was particularly fortunate for her. This city, located on the Mediterranean Sea in north-west Algeria has always been noted for its striking beauty, facing the sea and surrounded by lush, beautiful mountains. It had known Roman, Moorish, Castilian, Ottoman and Spanish rule. In 1831 Algeria was taken over by the French who ruled Oran and all of Algeria well into the twentieth century. However, in May and June, 1940, France fell to the Nazis.

At the same time most of the French Navy (Marine Nationale) were in the port of Mers-el-Kébir, quite near Oran. Fearful that the Nazis would also take control of all of those French ships in this port, Churchill ordered the bombardment of all of the French ships at Mers-el- Kébir on July 3, 1940, as part of the larger British war movement, "Operation Catapult." It didn't matter to Churchill that France had once been a staunch ally, not if most of the French fleet might soon become a part of Nazi Germany. Such a takeover might ultimately lead to the fall of Great Britain. As P.M.H. Bell has written regarding Great Britain, "The times were desperate; invasion seemed imminent; and the British government simply could not afford to risk the Germans seizing control of the French fleet.... The predominant British motive was thus dire necessity and self-preservation."

And so the British bombed the French ships at Mers-el-Kébir, thus denying the Nazis the addition of French ships to its own sizeable navy. The price for this act was high. The British bombing at Mers-el-Kébir killed 1,297 French sailors and wounded 350 more. This British military action prompted Charles de Gaulle to tell Winston Churchill that instead of fighting the Germans, it might give the French "greater satisfaction to turn their guns on their historic rivals, the British."

On November 8, 1942 Great Britain and the United States worked together in an amphibious attack, called Operation Torch, against French North Africa. By the time Anna Hunter arrived in Oran, that entire area was controlled by the Allies. The threat of attack where she worked was practically nonexistent. And the major languages spoken in Oran were French and English – Anna was already fairly fluent in French. Her principal job was to provide R & R to American soldiers.

In her journal before arriving in Oran, Anna wrote about the war in general – what the French were doing, Germany's conquests, and opinions in the United States. She focused on the Big Picture. Following her arrival in Oran, Anna narrowed her focus in her journal. She concentrated on her job – to provide respite to soldiers most of whom had either been or would soon be engaged in a hideous, all-pervasive war. Her job was not to analyze war strategies or philosophize. Instead, her assignment was to give these soldiers some relief from the horrors of war, and even in the process, to have perhaps some fun.

Most historians and students of literature agree that one of the greatest novels of World War II is *La Pest (The Plague),* by French writer and philosopher Albert Camus. In this work the plague, which is relentless in its attacks on the quarantined city's population, symbolizes World War II. Camus sets his entire novel in Oran, where he juxtaposes the silent beauty of that city with the horrors of death and hopeless struggle under a relentless blue sky, which resembles an eye, silently watching the drama below. One word appears repeatedly throughout this work: *Recommençons* (Let us begin again.) On a much smaller scale Anna was also inviting her "boys," as she called them, to begin again – to live in the now, to enjoy, laugh, sing, drink and play together in a safe environment – and most of all to remove, if only briefly, all thoughts of the war from their minds. And of course Anna was herself about to begin again. No longer was she just a poor widow from a small Southern town. She was free to re-create herself. And she did.

Her commanding officers gave her great leeway. She had an area, a building, a snack bar, assistants, a budget and the freedom to do almost anything she wished in order to provide battle-worn soldiers with badly-needed R and R. As she often stated in her journal, when she had a really good day, she generally ended her entry with the following: "We had fun!" Or sometimes, "They had fun!" Fun, diversion from the horrors of war, if only for a brief period, that was really Anna's central duty. She proved to be perfect for the job.

Formally, Anna was assigned to the Eighth Replacement Center, Camp OStelle, located in the Algerian countryside, not far from Oran. Her first opportunity to explore her new camp was on December 11, 1943 and she said, "It is on the side of a mountain and commands a view which is beautiful." Her new home was a Nissen Hut. *Wikipedia* describes this structure as "a prefabricated steel structure, made from a half-cylindrical skin of corrugated steel . . . used extensively during World War II." Those

Nissen Hut

who have lived in this structure have described it as a man-made cave, dark, damp, cold, with heavy blackout curtains at the windows and lighting only by one or two bulbs. As many as twelve soldiers could live in the Nissen Hut, which would contain no tables or chairs but only six bunk beds. Anna's description is quite different. "We have a living room with leather furniture – & a bedroom & 2 staff assistants and a bathroom with wash basin and a john – the privy type like a throne!" She described her new quarters as "marvelous!" Her only complaint was that the rainy season was starting and the hut was damp and cold. She most often ate at the officers' club and found the food there to be "delicious."

She soon became friends with generals and colonels, and when she requested some Christmas greenery, they promptly took her up into the mountains. "Went to French family and they promised all we wanted. Big farm – but the women and children in rags." She got her greens, but the firewood was too expensive.

She visited the lines and lines of hospital tents and described the scene as "bleak." She felt sorry for the women assigned there – and, of course, the men. Although much of her area had not yet been built (the snack bar was still outside), the troops began to take an interest in Anna's comings and goings. She received lots of help from the men, and soon lines began to form early for her club's programs. She described her "boys" sitting at a program, holding their helmets and with wet feet and was glad that they were at least for a brief time away from the bombs and bullets.

As Christmas neared, Anna decorated the shabby club with all sorts of greenery and flowers. She marveled at all the flowers blooming in December in Algeria. Enormous geraniums grew along the side of the road, along with other varieties. Anna noted in particular the beautiful star of Bethlehem. By December 24 her club was filled with "oranges, greens, trees, carols, and fudge." Christmas was "swell. Ate turkey and champagne." She had a wonderful time with the Colonel and stayed out until 3:00 a.m.

The month of January was quite busy for Anna. Although the buildings she used for her club were temporary, she decided that she should place permanent plants and landscape her surroundings. On January 22 she wrote, "Went out with Col. S's chauffeur Arnold with car and trailer (Arnold likes to run me around) – also 6 x 6 trailer and Italians [i.e. prisoners]. We went to Sidi Bel Okha for dirt – got chief of police to tell us where we could get it; . . . We all dug & got plants & came home & planted. Tried cactus on rocks in front." She never seemed to lack for help. A soldier who before the war had been a New York florist helped her decorate the club with huge branches of mimosa for a depot party. Later she wrote that the party was "swell."

On February 22nd she wrote: "Went to a cocktail party with col. At gen Wilson's villa – very swanky affair – beautiful villa all done over – Arab blankets etc. – Italian orchestra played. Gen Rogers who presided announced *Star Spangled Banner* and Italians played it – very impressive & so funny – enemies at <u>war</u>! Refreshments were elaborate and amazing. However hors-d'oeuvres were disguised C rations – little chunks of spam and cheese on toothpicks."

In spite of all the activity, talks, parties, and laughter, her "boys" soon had to depart. "They leave with their gear on & we know it is the real thing." Always there is this knowledge that these soldiers will soon be in battle again. But she never let the sadness she felt show. It would not have been fair to the new club arrivals.

Even before Anna got her assignment with the Red Cross, she had often expressed that she wanted to show what she could do. Her work at the camp near Oran, and later elsewhere tends to prove that she could not have been better placed in the war in order to prove not only what she could do, but how she could help others, whether it be a soldier with shellshock (today called post-traumatic stress disorder, PTSD), or serious physical injury. Although Anna had to answer to her superiors, they left her basically alone. They liked her and her work with the troops in particular. She lived in the present, trying to make each day the best she could. In Savannah during the war she had abhorred whiners and complainers, and in her service she refrained from pointing out the negative.

She was a self-starter, and her ideas were good. Her gregarious nature, her sense of humor, and her energy were a perfect match for the work she did with "her boys" and with her superiors. Whenever she needed help with any project, she got it – often many times over. Sometimes in Savannah, Anna did not get the recognition she wanted. She did not have the money to keep up with a society life style. And she did not have a husband at a time when much of Savannah high society was based on couples. In the war she hobnobbed with the lowest private and the highest commanders, eating in the officers' club and often going out with generals and colonels. No rank made her uncomfortable.

She also had an eye – for beauty, for style, for comfort. She designed the club and the snack bar at her camp near

Oran. And she took what she got and made something out of it. Her club was not made of brick or stone. The club itself was made of four prefabricated edifices put together. Yet she designed how these structures were to be put together and how the interior should look. She did not care if her building would remain after the war or be demolished. She wanted something for now – that would be inviting. Her designs worked, even her makeshift landscaping made the buildings look more permanent and certainly enhanced their beauty.

Anna had made personal strides toward the concept of racial equality in her days as a newspaper reporter in Savannah. For example, she wrote on January 6th, 1943, "George Washington Carver died today [actually he died on January 5th, 1943]. I wrote an editorial & it came to me with a shock that I had once passed up an interview with him fearing it would be awkward. I had a bad time today regretting that I could ever have felt so."

On January 19th, 1943 she wrote, "I was told I was to drive . . . a group of Negroes to Bare to sing next week. Good Cartoon – 1940 Society girl in limousine – colored chauffeur. 1943 society girl chauffeur with . . . negroes on backseat. Her Algerian assignment served to broaden her perspective and to see the intelligence and beauty of individuals, whether black or white or in between. As she aged the artistic part of Anna Hunter started blooming.

Of course there were negatives to her job. The biggest negatives were:

1. Saying goodbye to the soldiers and knowing where they would be going. "We lost big part of staff today. Big shipment going out. . . . We don't know what score is. But when we see boys leave here it is so close to war."

2. Anna's own illness in the sometimes dramatic new climate. Throughout most of January and February Anna developed a severe cough and cold. She described the weather: "The weather is most amazing. Bleak winds sleet – sporadic sunshine. The temperature doesn't go so low but gets under skin – it does something to you – my cold and cough and pain in back continue."

3. Missing her family. If Anna did not receive letters from home on a regular basis, she got lonely, sad and worried. Family letters often served as her lifeline.

At some time during her stay in Africa, she started what would become a family tradition: "The Lemon." She enclosed an old dried up lemon in a Christmas package and somehow it began to go back and forth until no-one [sic.] anticipated who had the lemon or who was going to get it next. While in North Africa, Anna must have verified the impression the Arabs had of this "crazy American lady" who insisted that the market produce for her, not a beautiful fresh lemon, but an old dried up one, which she promptly sent to one of her daughters in the States.

4. What might be called today sexual harassment. As Anna put it, "We are all made love to over here and we get very tired of it. . . . "[I]t is such a problem. Men are lonely. They want women over here & it is almost a struggle to keep

them in line. Most of them are married, some are too young, but they go on falling in love and inevitably there is a reckoning."

In her war journal Anna does explain her main purpose of writing. "I have had such a life of impressions. I have devoted my diary largely to these." She explains that she has not written of intrigue, gossip, loves, "because I cannot put them down in black and white – and because, too, I don't know what might happen to me or my diary. It also would be difficult to go into it all . . ."

Chapter 7

Anna in Naples

In May 1944 Anna faced a tough decision. The outfit she was assigned to, the Eighth, was ordered to transfer to Italy. In her journal she wrote, "Am all stirred up over decision. Col has recommended we move with them. I want to & yet I have feeling I should stay. Maybe new field here & I love place and hate to desert R. C. [Red Cross] but I want to go forward. Hard to decide. . . . I have had so much done for me I feel I shouldn't keep on leaning on C.O.'s support – but guess I am a fool. Other A R C girls pull wires to go with outfits. Yet I feel I'd like to be independent and fight my own battles. We all probably go the way of all flesh and go. May never get there if not now." Four days later she wrote, "I'm in jitters over whether to push going with 8th. Want to, yet feel strong urge to stay here and maybe try for India later."

On June 11th the new club, with which Anna had been so occupied since its inception, was finally open. Anna commented, "Looked lovely with flowers, etc., still much to do. She had a new staff – this time all Italian, [prisoners?] and at the main part of the club it was still quite disorganized. They also had to deal with "uninvited guests." As Anna stated, "So many bats in new quarters they called it the Belfry!"

On August 8th, Anna got some different news. "I heard today I may be released and sent on foreign assignment in Italy. I am excited but want to go in more – nearer the front but I feel terribly sad over leaving. I have loved this club – seen it grow – and having so many vegetables. And yet so much wonderful cooperation. I love Africa – and the mountains." The following day she was informed that her new orders would be coming in shortly. Yet still her excitement was considerably dampened by the sorrow of leaving all the people she worked with.

Two weeks later (August 22nd) Anna wrote, "I am sitting at the airport – cannot realize I have spent my last night in Africa. It is strange that I can feel little excitement over going to new lands – my heart is really heavy over leaving. I have loved . . . mountains with that deep feeling one can have only for a place of which he has felt a part. Then there are ties which will … ." Then her train of thought was broken as her plane was announced: (called out now – up in air)

With that announcement her story took a new turn: "Later – Arrival in Naples – very exciting – saw Vesuvius – it looked like a quiet old man with a gaping mouth – driving thru outskirts N. lay so beautifully in valley – so obviously helpless beneath Vesu – nobody concerned about our arrival – billeted in Red X [Red Cross] buildg. I miss my club sorely."

Yet she attended two operas the following two days and purchased "a little oil of a Naples stairway and archway – very characteristic." On August 25th, 1944 she saw the depot. "I was disappointed. It was in a sheltered valley with mts. around. After the georgous views from Sain Mt. and lovely view here it is cramping to [see this view]."

Naples Waterfront

However, the following day she saw the site of the new club and liked it. "Building has interesting features." As for Naples itself, it was a "seething mass of soldiers." By the first part of September, she had fallen ill. "Had a chill last night & sick today – had doctor – says it's sand-flea fever. Feel horrible – ache & fever. Bored to death and afraid I won't be well in time to fix club. I can see Vesuvius from my bed, tho – seems so strange. No mail – miserably detached."

Although she attempted to start work, her "horrible affliction" prevented it. In addition during her days in bed, the mail had failed to catch up to her new location. "In depths because I've had no mail yet." By September 8th she was still in bed and "staggered" when she tried to walk.

On September 9th, she wrote, "Felt like giving up this morning. So much wrong – keep being disappointed over not getting furniture & no transportation & bedlam and passing buck at Hq. Spent hours arranging for furniture & messages went wrong and none came – depot doesn't want to give us men to paint and meant 'till huts done.' – also no mail & I am frantic. . . . I'm low."

After only a few days Anna's irrepressible spirit began to rise. She got two letters from home; learned that her daughter was going to have another baby. She also got a tent near her working area where she could "rest up and take time out." Her rising optimism is almost laughable, for example: "9/11 Today engaged Antonio. He looks like a dead-end kid but says he is an Egyptian! And can interpret. He is red headed and lame. I can't understand him and he apparently doesn't understand me but I think we can work it out." And apparently she did!

From September 15th until September 25th Anna worked constantly from 8:15 a.m. until 10:00 p.m. each day. She spent most of her time "utterly exhausted." On September 15th the club opened amid much fanfare and top brass, in spite of the fact that much of it was not finished. "Since then I have been trying to train our Italian staff and run club with the snack bar in terrible condition because we had no running water and kitchen not complete." In nearly all of her labors no one told her what to do. She just did it. In the course of this period she developed an eye for what would look good and what wouldn't. She even had the liberty to design the interior of her buildings. The result was comfortable, useful and pleasing.

By September 25th she reported, "Things are starting [to work out] now. The club is quite nice. Built of 4 huts put together . . . . It's been a mad, confusing and hopeless job for me. Had so many disruptions, but things are smooth at last."

The staff that she had was not exactly first rate. "The boys in the depot are mostly limited service – many psychological cases. We not only have to give much more time to them individually but have to be careful – they get mad over refusals which are legitimate and necessary – and some of them have the 'I've been to the front' complex." She also had some Italians, whom she described as "a handful." While some were smart and responsible, others were "hopeless." They ranged in age from quite old to quite young. She continued, "It's like a madhouse sometimes." Then with her usual optimism she said, "I enjoy them tho." She gave an example of the mayhem she often encountered: "The other night we had a Negro who was drunk and insisted on being served after hours. He caused a fuss for almost ½ hour – finally I asked M.P. to take him out. They were at the S Bding and I thought of course that they would go that way. To my horror M.P made a center dash and charged down the hall and thru the hall pushing the fellow ahead. The crowd closed in behind and at the door a soldier raised his voice objecting strenuously to having M.P. "bully" them. This caused quite a scene and was very nasty."

And of course the weather did not always co-operate: "It rained tonight and the club was a seething mass of humanity. There must have been 500 men in there at one time. The place is just too small for [such] numbers."

Anna received many congratulatory letters, verbal praise, commendations and certificates of merit for her work in Africa and Italy. On September 6, 1944 Colonel George S. Beatty wrote the following letter to Anna:

> I wish to officially commend you for your superior work as director of the Red Cross in my depot. You accomplished great things in spite of the terrible handicap that confronted you. From nothing you built up one of the finest Red Cross installations in Italy. In addition to your Red Cross activities, you were a most efficient and helpful Staff Officer, always giving me valuable information as to morale and the general condition of the command. . . . . 2. I have recommended you for the Bronze Star Medal for meritorious service and trust that it may be awarded. . . . 3. Wishing you further success and Happiness."

Although Colonel Beatty made this recommendation, Anna Hunter did not technically qualify for the Bronze Star, since it was reserved exclusively for members of the United States military.

Three months earlier, an Army Service paper in North Africa printed the following:

> We doff our khaki chapeau to Mrs. Hunter of the A.R.C. [American Red Cross] for being an all around good sport, and a grand morale builder. . . . Did you see her blasting with a bazooka at the demonstration on Lion Mt. last Saturday? And she hit her target too, and old arthritic tank. . . . After such a demonstration we fellows should feel capable of handling a bazooka in like manner. . . . I understand she is an excellent rifle shot, and I KNOW she plays a

swell game of ping-pong. . . . This beside her numerous activities in her regular channel of work. Our thanks to the A.R.C. in the U.S.A. for sending us Mrs. Hunter and her aides . . .

In 1945 Anna took a badly needed vacation. Exactly where she went is not known, except that she visited Switzerland. She then returned to Italy and left from there to the United States to go to her daughter's wedding in Mobile, Alabama. Even her departure was duly recorded by one of her soldier-fans:

> I have this day bid our Anna C. Hunter farewell and *bon voyage.* Tomorrow she departs from Sunny Italia for the U.S. If I were a commanding general of the U.S. Army (not just serial number ------) I would give her the Congressional Medal of Honor. I believe that she has done more to make the G.I. in this theatre of operations happy than any other person. All her work has been in clubs in replacement depots where the men do practically nothing but sit around and wait . . . . You can't imagine what the problems involved in the administration of one of these clubs are. She has overcome them all. Her work should be noted and recorded in some way. It was a magnificent contribution to the war in this theatre.

Anyone who looks at her record can see that she accomplished a great deal during her stays in Africa and Italy. What might not be so readily clear is what she received from her experience.

From the moment the United States entered World War II, Anna wanted to do something significant for the war effort. When she was assigned to Naples, she wished that her assignment had been nearer to the front. Often, she spoke about her facilities and her snack bar. It was not just a tiny place serving the needs of dozens. As Colonel Beatty said, "During November [1944] 70,027 men used the snack bar and it is estimated that between 225,000 and 250,000 men use the Red Cross facilities each month." And Anna was in charge of some of those facilities. Her job was huge, and she had no particular direction from anyone else. She could have made her job nearly anything she wanted.

First, she set out to try to make any soldier there comfortable and, at least for the moment, relaxed. She played ping pong (and often won); she danced, she sang, she was sometimes a soda jerk; she laughed; she designed the facilities; and she often made, or searched for items to decorate her domain. But most of all she had fun, the kind of fun that was contagious, even (and especially) affecting battle-worn soldiers. Her work was invaluable.

Second. She came in contact with people of all types, colors, languages and rank. She worked with generals all the way down to prisoners of war. Not only could she get things done, she could persuade. High ranking officers loaned her their drivers to go into town or the mountains to obtain supplies and/or decorations for her facility. She dined with officers, worked with privates, and played ping pong with sergeants. Or vice versa.

Third. She admired the buildings and houses of Oran and Naples, some of them hundreds of years old, along with their cultures. She came to appreciate how residents changed the interiors of their dwellings without disturbing the exteriors.

She admired antiquity and realized that modern was not always better than old.

Fourth. She got to know many different types of men. Although she complained that too many of "her boys" became too attracted to her, she was often the center of attention and sometimes even adulation. She was not only often in the spotlight, but became a central figure for planning and implementing new ideas for her facility. There is no doubt that she enjoyed the notoriety. And her insights and conceptions worked.

A fifth "skill" that Anna developed in the course of her work in Africa and Italy was the fact that by the time she returned to the states, she could drink just about anyone under the table.

Anna came home to Savannah in December, 1944, a far more learned and experienced woman than she was when she left for Africa two years earlier. No longer was she a poor, old provincial widow living in relative isolation in the deep South. She was a woman to be reckoned with, as Savannah would soon discover.

Chapter 8

Anna's Return to Savannah

Upon her return to Savannah, Anna resumed her job first at the *Savannah Evening Press* and later the *Morning News*. She at first worked as a local reporter, but was then given more and more jobs within the society pages. In that realm she covered the arts: painting, theater, lectures, and often books in the Sunday supplement. She continued to attend nearly every concert, play or other theatrical performance that came to Savannah. In addition, her column, "Nobody's Business," which recorded the comings and goings of prominent Savannahians became popular and lasted for decades.

When Anna sang in church and in musicals, she harbored a desire to become an opera singer. And when Anna worked on the newspaper staff, she hoped to become a famous Southern novelist. While doing lesser jobs in both areas, she always seemed to be looking toward the top, the best, the most significant.

At first Anna rented a small, inexpensive apartment on Jones Street in Savannah. However, by 1947 she viewed her residence with dissatisfaction. To Anna it was dull, too small and unattractive. She eyed the huge warehouses along the river that once held cotton, the Cotton Exchange and the cotton factors (brokers who set worldwide cotton prices). The warehouses were now mostly empty – virtually abandoned. She took particular note of Factors Walk, which sat on a bluff overlooking the cobblestones of River Street and the river below. Part of a warehouse at 230 East Bay Street was for rent. Exuberant, she rented it against the outcries of nearly all of her friends and acquaintances. They believed her new quarters were too dangerous, particularly for a woman alone, frequented below on River Street by drunks, thieves, wayward sailors and evildoers. But Anna was undeterred. Besides, the rent was "affordable" – in other words, dirt cheap. While Anna was in Algeria and Italy, she purchased many interesting pieces of pottery and paintings. At the time she was able to ship these items at little or no expense to Georgia. She decorated the long brick walls of her new place with these objects. And there was plenty of room for more.

Now something else slowly crept into her mind: art – painting. Years ago when she attended Agnes Scott College, she had plenty of opportunities to take classes in art. Yet her transcripts and yearbooks reveal that she didn't take advantage of this possibility. Instead she enjoyed just about any sport that was offered at this small college, and was good in all of them. She also participated in drama and singing; she wrote poetry and prose; she belonged to many clubs, had lots of friends and loved the many parties that always seemed to be popping up.

But art? Back then she never seemed to have the time or inclination.

However, Anna had changed considerably since those girlhood days. Her exposure to art and architecture abroad expanded almost exponentially along with her exposure to new cultures. She loved art, whether by an unschooled native or a master – all piqued her interest – and often her admiration. Back in the States the course of her profession as a reporter also influenced her art interest. As part of her job Anna became the paper's art critic, with or without experience. In music, drama, and writing she had experience and was confident of her knowledge. But in art? Could she really critique a visiting artist or art show if she had no experience at all in that area? To try to remedy this situation, she began to draw, to paint, to explore art starting with the

Hunter in Savannah, After the War

basics. She loved it. As she would have said a few years earlier, she was "thrilled."

In the late 1940s and early 1950s we find Anna working hard as a newspaper reporter, society editor, and the paper's critic of arts and letters. Several people have described her rushing into the press room and pounding away on her typewriter. And here and there we see Anna hard at work on her newspaper columns in unusual places, such as the following:

> A few nights ago, returning with friends form (sic. from) the country, the car broke down midway to town. Mrs. Hunter had one more book to review for her column, and there was nothing she could do to help, so out came the book, the top light was switched on and there she sat reading away against time and the deadline. Passersby must have been amazed at such avidity for knowledge. Cars whizzed by, mechanics banged away, but she got her column finished.

In addition, she began to establish what would become a significant career of her own in art. To have these two careers at the same time required a huge expenditure of work. Logically, she should not have taken on anything more. But something else caught her eye and was invading her town with all the sinister inevitability of that old boll weevil. It was slowly but surely decimating the town with even more finality and ferocity than that cotton-loving bug: ROT. The town was rotting from the inside out. And just like the initial reaction to the boll weevil, no one really noticed . . . until it was almost too late.

As has been seen, during World War II, Savannah was busy, as was its port, and there was plenty of money to go around. Immediately following the War, however, nearly everything in Savannah either slowed or stopped, and once again money became scarce. Nobody thought much about Savannah's Historic District with its beautiful homes and well-kept gardens. In fact those homes were no longer beautiful since most residents had moved away. And what was that smell? It permeated nearly the whole town. Some natives of Savannah referred to it as "Savannah Perfume." Actually, it was the stench of raw sewage flowing freely from the town into the Savannah River. This sour odor was heavily spiced with the acrid smell of the paper mill.

In 1946, Lady Astor visited Savannah and described it as, "*a beautiful*

Lady Astor

lady with a dirty face. Although the city was shocked by Astor's pronouncement, no one attempted to remedy the situation. In fact, further deterioration continued. Historians Preston Russell and Barbara Hines later wrote that if Lady Astor had seen Savannah in the 1950s, she might have described its face as "ravaged by smallpox." What is now called the Historic District had become mostly a slum, with broken windows, weeds, mold, rats, and rampant abandonment. Needless to say, housing prices plunged. Larger homes were sometimes divided into tenement housing for the poor and destitute. No one seemed to want to invest in what was fast becoming Savannah's hell hole. There seemed to be nothing of value there – with one exception: the bricks. The beautiful bricks that were used to erect many of those old houses were handmade, rare, and costly. It seemed logical to just tear down the houses and cart off the bricks for use in new homes and buildings. To many Savannahians at that time the most useful tool to beautify the so-called Historic District was the wrecking ball. Raze the buildings, take the bricks, replace the old squares with thoroughfares and the historic edifices with parking lots and be done with it. Why not?

But even razing the structures required money – more money than most investors were willing to pay. There was no grand plan for the new development of the Historic District. As Russell and Hines state, "*Savannah was too poor to destroy itself.*"

As retired Superior Court Judge Perry Brannen stated regarding Savannah's Historic District, "The largest urban historic district in the United States has survived because, fortunately, the poor economy back then would not allow its replacement. In a sense, Savannah's history has preserved the history we see today."

However, no plan had yet been made for the Historic District's preservation. A single person might purchase a house and restore it, while another three houses in the same area simply disappeared. Often the permits and/or bills allowing the demolition of a building quietly passed city hall or state government. By the time Savannah's residents heard of the new plans, it was often too late to save the edifice. The shock, dismay, and sorrow at the loss of another dwelling served no purpose. The wrecking ball had won again.

There was a rationale that justified Savannah's divesting itself of everything in the city that was old. "Out with the old and in with the new" became the motto of much of the South in this era. The southern states tended to give themselves an important and defining adjective: NEW, as in the NEW South. Most southerners believed that they had bemoaned the loss of the Civil War and looked with nostalgia at their past long enough. It was time to look with hope toward the future, which would have new ideas, more money, and brand new homes and buildings. If some questioned this logic, they had only to look to Atlanta. New buildings and businesses were popping up like mushrooms all over that city. It seems that whenever a building got old, Atlantians gave it to the wrecking ball, torn down and replaced by a new, better, more beautiful edifice that somehow exemplified Atlanta's bright future. Modern is better in Atlanta – always better, wiser, and more efficient.

Many Savannahians wanted to use Atlanta as the model for their city. What few people considered, however, or even remembered was Atlanta's past. Sherman had just about destroyed anything of value in Atlanta before the Civil War. There were few, if any, old buildings to save. And what about Savannah's once-beautiful squares? They might be full of weeds and brambles now, but everyone had to admit that they held promise for beautiful, spacious green areas right downtown – or the promise of turning those squares into parking lots to encourage downtown parking.

Yet almost no one could fault the city's original plan, laid out in orderly squares by Oglethorpe in 1733, with additional squares added all the way up to 1866. The plan did not originate with Oglethorpe, but dates from ancient Greece. Each square consisted of open space in the center, with four trust lots on each corner. These trust lots were meant for the most imposing structures, whether churches, impressive buildings or mansions. Behind them was a systematic arrangement of lots, houses, carriage houses and lanes. The whole square was orderly, balanced. There were 2.2 square miles of these squares within the heart of the city. Adding or subtracting from any one of them in a new way or pattern would clash and destroy the square's harmony. No other city in the nation had such an area. "Residences for rich and poor, young and old, are side by side with churches, schools, shops, stores, government buildings, businesses, professional offices and cultural facilities." Each square could accommodate pedestrians and/or automobiles. And the fact that Savannah is a seaport added to the diversity of its population and religious faiths, not to mention more tourist attractions.

Nearly everyone in Savannah realized that there were two sides regarding what to do with the historic part of Savannah, and each believed that their side would make a better future for their city. Some wanted to replace the entire area with the new and modern, while others wanted to preserve the beauty of their past. But talk was cheap. In the 1940s and early 1950s, no real plan for the future of this dismal area was developed on either side, and the rot, broken windows, theft of bricks and haphazard razing of buildings continued. "Of the fifty priceless Savannah buildings recorded in the federal government's Historic American Buildings Survey in 1934, fourteen would be demolished later."

Chapter 9

Founding the Historic Savannah Foundation

A smattering of restoration projects did succeed in haphazard fashion. For example, in 1945, Mrs. Hansell Hillyer, the wife of the chief executive of the Savannah Gas Company decided to restore several old clapboard cabins situated on the site of the old Trustees Garden. Her restoration resulted in a new neighborhood of attractive small homes that proved to be both attractive and profitable – to the astonishment of the town. However, others did not follow Mrs. Hillyer's example.

In 1951 two bills from Savannah were presented to the Georgia General Assembly. The first bill would have permitted the city to change Habersham Street into a through boulevard, running across several squares and going from Bay Street to Victory Drive. That bill got the town's attention and resulted in the creation of the Society for the Preservation of the Squares of Savannah. During the fight to stop any attempt to ruin Savannah's squares, the other bill was overlooked and passed through the General Assembly largely unnoticed. This bill permitted the city of Savannah to convert the large, beautiful, and often-used old City Market into a parking garage. Many businessmen believed that if more parking could be found, more shoppers would come to the many shops on Broughton Street instead of frequenting nearby malls.

City Market, early 1900's

The location of the City Market had been established as a place to sell fresh vegetables, fruit and seafood almost as far back as the founding of Georgia. The first food market was comprised of two buildings, both of which burned, one in 1788 and the other in 1820. A third market building was torn down following the Civil War, replaced in 1872 by a larger, more suitable building (the last). It was designed by two German architects: Martin Miller and Augustus Schwaab. "This splendid building dominated Ellis Square for over eighty years. It was a cavernous ornate brick structure with Romanesque-styled arches, large circular windows, and a soaring 50-foot roof line." Daily activity there was brisk, beginning in early morning with trucks, cars and mule-drawn wagons taking their spots, women loading baskets of vegetables or fruit for sale onto their heads and the sing-song calls of people (then called hucksters) with pushcarts hawking their wares. As one who knew the City Market well, Freeman Jelks, Jr. stated in 2005:

> It was a real city market. Black people sold stuff – things like vegetables and possums. We could consider it charming today. At the time there were health concerns. It had horrific odors. There were health concerns by the Health Department. As a journalist I was aware of city officials. The Health Department Director, Dr. Claire Henderson, told me the city would have had to close it [if it were not torn down]. It had no sanitation at all.

The workers at the old City Market generally brought their children along. The sidelines held fierce games of marbles, babies napping in the shade, dirt roads decorated with hopscotch grids, old men engrossed in checkers, and mules (often wearing straw hats with holes cut for the ears to shade their faces). Yellow tail, flounder, bass, shrimp, drum, all kinds of seafood fresh from the sea vied with fresh tomatoes, butterbeans, corn, collards, persimmons, cherries, peaches, melons and figs for notice from the busy customers. The City Market was one of the liveliest, most colorful places in Savannah touting great prices and food. Blacks and whites freely associated in the buying and selling of goods.

In 1952, however, Anna started to face a much more serious problem for her than the future of the old City Market. Her only son George Jr. was in bad health. Anna had worried about him ever since her husband's death in 1936. George Jr. was a sensitive young man who was sometimes overwhelmed by the three strong and assertive women remaining in his family. He had considerable artistic talent. Accomplished artist Henry Lee McPhee mentored him and when he moved to California, George followed him there in 1938. He married, had two children and taught art classes for emotionally disturbed youth at the Devereux Schools. He also wrote a book on art that was never published.

George was building a house in Santa Barbara when his shoulder began to cause him great pain, later diagnosed as a sarcoma of the joint in his shoulder. Although he was given a shoulder girdle amputation, the cancer had already spread. He died of lung metastases on November 21, 1952, at the age of thirty-four. Had it not been for a special donation for Anna from the members of her church, she could not have gone to California to be with him during his last operation and subsequent death.

Upon her return to Savannah following her son's funeral, Anna kept her grief mostly to herself. Instead of expressing her personal sorrow, she plunged into her newspaper work and took up again the cause of preservation in Savannah with renewed vigor, particularly regarding the old City Market. But her preservation efforts were doomed. Reflecting upon the destruction of the market, Anna stated, "The sting of this demolition was that in the last minute the purchasers told the group trying to save it that they would hold off if a constructive use could be found for it." But the opposition, disorganized and random, was not yet ready to provide such a plan. By the time the protest against the market's demolition got into full swing, it was too late. Instead, in October, 1953, Anna Colquitt Hunter headed the group that threw that magnificent old structure a farewell – in the form of a gala costume ball. Each participant was to go dressed as something that was sold at the market. Winner of the prize for the most original costume was Emory Jarrott. "With red balloons all over his body and a red cap, he waddled in as a bunch of radishes."

Anna was not the only one to feel sorrow the night of the ball. Emma and Lee Adler later said, "We returned from our wedding trip in the fall of 1953 in time to attend a costume ball – the 'last hurrah' for Savannah's City Market. We were outraged that this substantial building, which had flourished in Ellis Square since 1888 would be demolished in 1954 to be replaced by a parking garage built by the city with support from downtown merchants to accommodate shoppers and attract them away from a new strip-shopping area on East Victory Drive at Skidaway Road. The demolition of the market would constitute an irreplaceable loss."

Nevertheless, what came after the old City Market's demolition may have awakened many citizens to stark reality. "A particularly sterile parking garage now sits there like a thumb in the city's eye." At that time Anna vowed that never again would a building or home fall to the wrecking ball without a coordinated fight. The fall of the City Market had to be the last time that bills to change or destroy Savannah's wonderful old buildings would slip by unnoticed. As Anna later explained it:

> One evening I went to dinner at the Reuben Clarks [his wife's name was Katherine, but

everyone called her Kass] and approached them on the idea of organizing a preservation group. Kass was already interested in the Owens-Thomas House, as was Jane Wright who was present. When I suggested the names of persons who might participate, Reuben, with characteristic dispatch, said, "Why not call them now?" That evening and the next morning calls resulted in the acceptance of four persons in addition to Kass, Jane and myself.

In less than twenty-four hours, Anna had invited six other people to join her in her nascent group. They were:

1. Jane Adair Wright, 1901 - 1993, born in Hillsborough, Ohio.

2. Katherine Judkins Clark, 1897 – 1992, born in Danville, Virginia.

3. Lucy Barrow McIntire, 1886 - 1967, born in Athens, Georgia.

4. Dorothy Ripley Roebling, 1904-1977, born in Essex, New Jersey.

5. Elinor Grunsfeld Adler {Dillard}, 1903 – 1992, born in New York.

6. Nola McEvoy Roos, 1895 – 1980, born in Georgia.

For details about these six women, please see Appendix A.

Anna Colquitt Hunter and her six hand-picked cohorts formed the union that became the Historic Savannah Foundation in 1955. Looking more closely at this initial group, one sees that its members were entirely composed of women – old or relatively old women. The youngest woman Dorothy Ripley Roebling was born in 1904. In 1955, they ranged in age from 51 to 69. However, from the beginning these women intended to include men after the original plans had been set in place. As Lucy McIntire later stated, "We . . . had the good sense to appeal to the male contingent. . . . None of us sought office but approached leading [male] citizens in the industrial and business world."

Most of the businessmen at that time tended to view the restoration of old buildings as aesthete, certainly not practical – an expensive hobby. No one at that time, not even the seven women of the Historic Savannah Foundation, saw the huge potential that tourism could provide. In fact when the seven ladies prepared a list of the six goals they hoped to attain, the very last one was "tourism" – almost placed within their list of goals as a hopeful sigh. The five goals placed before tourism seemed somehow more important. They were:

1. Formulation of a long range program of preservation and restoration with emphasis on the original city plan

2. Professional advice

3. Survey of downtown Savannah

4. Practical use of buildings saved

5. Zoning measures

Then came number 6, the shortest of all, and the last goal – just one word. 6. Tourism. Who would have ever guessed that tourism would soon become the second largest industry in Savannah, second only to the Savannah seaport? Within a relatively short period of time Savannah tourism turned from a less than $100,000 a year business to more than a billion dollar industry with millions of tourists each year. In 2016, for example, there were 13.9 million total visitors to Savannah. 7.9 million visitors stayed overnight. The total expenditure of those overnight tourists was $2.23 billion, a figure that was unimaginable in the 1950s.

It was probably wise that these women waited until they had established their little foundation on a stronger footing before they asked the men to help them. Many of the men (and some women) referred to their group as "The Hysterical Society."

All but one of the seven women were married or widowed. More surprising is the fact that none of these women was originally from Savannah – and only two were from the state of Georgia. Most of these ladies came to Savannah as brides. Except for Anna, few had loving childhood memories of Savannah to cause them to become preservationists.

The education level of the original founders of the Historic Savannah Foundation was also unusual. The 1940 census shows that all of these women graduated from high school; two had two years of college experience, and three graduated from college – all from excellent educational facilities. In 1940 only 3.8% of the adult women in the nation had graduated from college. In fact, less than 30% of all adult white women in the United States had completed high school in 1940.

All of them with one exception ranged in income from well to do to quite rich. That one exception was Anna Colquitt Hunter. Again, according to the 1940 census, she worked forty-eight hours a week, fifty two weeks per year – for the salary of $1330 per year (equal to a little over $22,000 in 2017). And in 1940 her rent was $25.00 per month. (In all likelihood because she was the first to rent part of an old warehouse in the 1950s, her rent was probably the same or less at that time). In that regard she led the way, since the use of a warehouse for a studio or an apartment was not yet chic. As for those women who received some salary, all made more than Anna in 1940, and had other sources of income. Those who rented paid more than twice or three times as much as Anna. And some of these owned or rented more than one residence.

Dorothy Roebling's house was valued on the 1940 census at $25,000. That does not count their fabulous schooner, *Black Douglas*, they also lived on during their stay on nearby Skidaway Island. In addition to the cable company, used in the building of some of the nation's largest bridges, they also had other holdings: the Modena Plantation and a business partnership in the Mercer Automobile Company a sports/race car shop in Savannah. When Robert Roebling retired, he gave each member of his family a sports car of his/her own.

All of these women agreed that it was the destruction of the Old City Market in 1953-54 which served as the catalyst to start a Savannah preservation group. Regarding the ball which served as a send-off of the Old City Market, Savannahian Emory Jarrot later said : "It was really ironic in a way. There was a feeling of resignation, but at the same time there was this determination that had started to grow, as if losing the market were the last straw. It was a disaster, but from the disaster grew Historic Savannah."

It is clear that the original seven women forming the Historic Savannah Foundation were unusually bright and amazingly determined. They had broad experience; knew how to get things done, liked each other, and shared one goal: preservation of the historic part of Savannah. Most of the group had worked well with the other group members. They wanted the surprise that came when the Old City Market was slated to be demolished to be their last. Nothing else must slip by. Right from the first, through serious deliberation they started to develop a plan. As Anna later said, "A meeting was set for my studio and we were off in a cloud of dust – I might say gunpowder." At that time they decided that their major goal was to set a long-range plan. However, the first order of business had to be to educate every Savannahian about the treasure that Savannah's old homes and buildings represented. They weren't just old garbage to be thrown out. Other Georgian towns did not have such a fine and unusual collection of American architecture, most of which lined the wonderful squares, now unkempt, that James Oglethorpe had originally designed. It was time to sweep the cobwebs and filth off the amazing center buildings of their town, some of which dated back to the founding of the colony of Georgia. As Preston Russell and Barbara Hines stated:

> Between 1900 and 1955 the wealth of magnificent architecture in the historic district was generally ignored. Demolition joined decay in taking its toll. The priceless buildings represented a succession of architectural styles: Federal, English Regency, Classical Revival, Italian Villa, Gothic Revival, Romantic Revival, Second Empire – Savannah had supported them all. Classic buildings by William Jay, John Norris, Charles B. Clusky, William Gibbons Preston, and A. E. Eichberg were being lost.

The people of Savannah needed to realize what they had in their own backyards. The education of Savannah's citizenry was crucial to the success of any preservation project. And while that instruction was proceeding, the Seven Ladies would also develop a long-range plan, taking into consideration all of the ramifications of such a preservation project. As soon as possible, they needed to take steps to prevent any more demolition bills from passing through the state and local halls of government unnoticed: NO MORE SURPRISES!

Chapter 10

Growth of the Historic Savannah Foundation

SURPRISE! Before the seven could launch their educational program, and certainly before any other plans were initiated, another ugly surprise swept in. It all seemed to start innocently enough. Katherine Summerlin purchased the Isaiah Davenport House, a Federal-style home built around 1820. It was the oldest brick structure left in the city. At the time of her purchase, this 6,800 square-foot house had become tawdry and ramshackle.

Good for Ms. Summerlin! Maybe she intended to restore it. It was not until the Seven Ladies learned just who Katherine Summerlin was and what she intended to do with the structure that they gasped in horror. She was the step-daughter of Mr. Goette, the owner of the thriving Goette Funeral Home near the Davenport House. Summerlin bought the Davenport estate for her step-father. And he had no restoration plans. He intended to raze the place to

Left: Davenport House, c. 1940

Below: Davenport House, c. 2000

accommodate the parking needs of his increasing number of grieving visitors, and sell off all of the bricks.

At the time of Summerlin's purchase of the house, it had become a virtual tenement. Journalist Freeman Jelks admitted that the Davenport was located in a dangerous area. "You just did not go there. The area was a slum." Having lived all his life in Savannah, he admitted that he had never even seen this house until he was twenty-six years old. When he did visit this disreputable tenement, he reported:

> I went down to the Davenport House to see it for myself. When I went in the stink was appalling. And I had smelled some pretty bad stuff – having been in the army in Japan during the Korean War. The janitor's basin (under the stair on the first floor) was used as a urinal. There was no door on the janitor's closet . . .
>
> Ten tiny apartments were chopped out of it. Wooden partitions all around.

It is clear that the Davenport House was hardly a place to be championed by seven proper ladies. Yet immediately the Seven Ladies, leaped into action. As Jelks later noted, "There was no window dressing with the ladies." First they contacted Katherine Summerlin and asked her if she would be willing to sell the Davenport property to them. She was hesitant at first, but more than a parking lot, she just wanted to get rid of the Davenport eyesore so near to their business. "From her standpoint it was better to have a vacant lot than a slum across the street. That was bad for business." With the persuasiveness of Monsignor James McNamara, who loved downtown Savannah and the work of the Seven Ladies, a deal was struck.

Left: Foyer of Davenport House, c. 1950.

Below: Foyer of Davenport House, today.

If they paid her $22,500 before the date of the demolition, she would give them the deed to the property. The Seven Ladies then proceeded to canvass the town explaining what was going to happen to the Davenport House if the necessary funds were not raised in time, reminding the town of what happened to the City Market and pointing out what replaced it.

The foundation raised the funds only hours before the wrecking ball would have swung. Local lore reports that when the wrecker, accustomed to razing historic buildings for their bricks, asked Lee Adler, *Where do you want your bricks put?* He replied: *Just leave them where they are for now.* Restored by the fledgling Historic Savannah Foundation, the house became the symbol of Savannah's rebirth and eventually also the group's headquarters.

The first official meeting of the Savannah Historic Foundation occurred in Anna's studio/apartment in the spring of 1955. Seven determined ladies attended. Because of the intense public-relations campaign launched over the summer by Anna Hunter and her six cohorts, a stunning 700 people attended the Savannah Historic Foundation's first general membership meeting on November 9, 1955.

Margaret Minis, in her article "Artist's Portrait" in the *Georgia Gazette* describes Anna in those days: "Hunter accomplished such miracles through a combination of energy, wit and charm, plus the determination not to take 'no' for an answer, according to longtime friends."

"'I remember when she started,' recalled one. "'She called on me and asked me if I would support her if she ever needed help. Thinking she meant some vague time in the future, I said I'd be glad to. The next thing I knew she was telling me what my job was.'"

The objective of the HSF remained the same from the beginning and is stated in its original charter (also received in 1955): "Formulation of a long range program of preservation and restoration with emphasis on the original city plan." Next, they sought professional advice regarding how to proceed. They wrote to Boston, to the firm of Perry, Shaw, Hepburn, and Deen. These lawyers had helped with the restoration of Williamsburg and Old Salem. That firm sent a representative to Savannah to help HSF to develop its plan and to give advice as to possible actions and pitfalls.

As the women of the fledgling Historic Savannah Foundation launched their campaign to save the heart of the city from destruction, they seldom used the word "tourism" in their pitch. They realized that for many of the locals, "tourism" was not a good thing. In those days many Savannahians did not want to welcome others to their town. To have foreigners, worse for some, Northerners traipsing around their town, sticking their noses into everything, was initially just plain anathema. Let the Yankees stay up North! Many Savannahians agreed with the following poem that originated in Charleston, which at the time shared similar prejudices:

> May Day has come, we all rejoice,
> Once more the City's ours.
> The Yankees have departed
> With the early April flowers.

Anna and her six volunteers had taken on a difficult and complicated job: preservation, restoration, education, tourism, publicity, and donations – all this and so much more fell into their domain. Yet sources describing these women at the time leave the impression not of women overwhelmed – but rather of women overwhelming, accepting with enthusiasm all the tasks set before them. They even laughed at their local nickname, "The Hysterical Society," or being compared to a gaggle of "geese." Their smiles were more than justified, for not only were they doing a great job for Savannah's preservation, some of the biggest and most influential "ganders" in the city had already joined them.

The replacement of the old City Market by an ugly parking lot plus the threatened destruction of the once-beautiful Davenport House – both served as a catalyst for the citizens of Savannah. It had become clear to almost everyone that if they wanted to preserve anything of their city's past, they had to take action immediately, even if that meant that a few more tourists might come to their town. And so in 1955, the same year the HSF was founded, this infant organization raised enough money to purchase the Davenport House, thus saving it from demolition. In addition, what everyone realized at the time was that at the head of this preservation movement, its original instigator and tireless leader was Anna Colquitt Hunter. She founded the Historic Savannah Foundation and took the steps necessary to place it on a firm foundation. Its purpose never wavered from its inception to this day. In a speech Anna gave to the Friends of the Library in February,

1968, she stated, "It is my happy mission to tell you that those objectives which we outlined in the beginning have continued major goals through the years – and you cannot imagine the satisfaction of those who envisioned them to witness the fruition of some of those ideas and the continued effort toward other of these goals . . . not on an amateur scale but on a tremendous scale with a dynamic organization and professional execution."

The first president of the Historic Savannah Foundation was Jack Rauers, followed by Hansell Hillyer, Anna C. Hunter, and Albert Stoddard. Although this delineation comes from the words of Anna Hunter herself in her speech to the Friends of the Library, Lee and Emma Alder, in their book *Savannah Renaissance,* give their presidential delineation as Anna Colquitt Hunter (1955-1956), Jack Rauers (1956-1958), H. Hansell Hillyer (1958-1959), and Albert H. Stoddard (1959-1961). In any event by all accounts these four people provided excellent stewardship for the fledgling organization and took steps to make it more and more professional. In short, from 1955 to 1961 the following were saved: the Davenport House, the Lachlan McIntosh House, the Francis Stone house, Emmett Park, and Marshall Row (four gray brick Savannah row houses). In addition, other projects were launched, such as making a detailed survey of the buildings, outbuildings, streets, squares, and parks of the area. Throughout this period the HSF emphasized that profit was not their main goal, but rather putting "the buildings into the hands of those who would restore them . . . ." Sometimes it took a long time for the HSF to purchase a house in danger of demolition and hold it until a suitable buyer could be found who would restore the property, and sometimes it happened quickly. In addition, Savannah Mayor Malcom Maclean pledged to provide notification of all future demolition permits and a waiting period before granting the permits, thereby giving the HSF more time to take action.

Nearly everyone who held significant positions in the young HSF agreed that one man, who chose not to hold office in this organization, provided invaluable support to this fledgling group: Walter Charlton Hartridge. As Anna stated, Hartridge, a Harvard graduate, ". . . was a bulwark of strength not only in his role of incomparable historian but in year-in, year-out dedication, financial aid and courageous undertakings." In writing about this man, authors Emma and Lee Adler conclude that Hartridge, ". . . cared passionately about every building, street, square, and cobblestone in downtown Savannah, and long before there was any significant, well-organized preservation movement in Savannah, Walter Hartridge's efforts in the field of historic preservation constituted a one-man movement." Another huge initial supporter of the causes of the Historic Savannah Foundation was Reuben Clark, the husband of one of the original Seven Ladies, Katherine Clark. As Anna later wrote, "He was a pillar of strength being interested from the beginning – and when you have interest plus a bank – that counts."

In these years walking and river tours were inaugurated, as were lectures to Savannah's citizens regarding the advantages of tourism. The HSF stressed to its citizens that in Savannah tourists, even Yankees, would not be seeking to re-enact Civil War battles, where the South always lost, as happened in other parts of the South. Instead, what tourists would want to see in Savannah was the architectural and cultural beauty of Savannah's and therefore the South's past. Tourists would come to Savannah to admire it, not to belittle it.

Five years after the inception of the HSF, Albert Stoddard, who would serve as president of that organization, made the following remark to the *Savannah Morning News:*

> Historic Savannah Foundation has been operating for five years and has grown from a nucleus of seven women to 1200 members. We have brought the beauty and rare character of old Savannah to the attention of the community and changed the attitude of the public from apathy to appreciation of the importance of preserving things which can never, even with wealth, be recaptured.

In the spring of 1961 a truly remarkable person became president of HSF. Anna describes it like the setting for a play:

> This brings us up to the spring of 1961. ENTER DYNAMO! Lee Adler. It is not often that a burgeoning civic project has the good fortune to have the man of the hour loom on the horizon at a crucial hour.

While it would be too long to describe all of Adler's accomplishments during his five-term reign as president of HSF, his key achievements were:

1. Changing the HSF from an amateur civic organization into big business. Under Adler's leadership, the HSF secured its first professional director: Picot Floyd, highly capable, who later became Savannah's City Manager.

2. Launching and implementing the Revolving Redevelopment Fund. This fund provided $200,000, which enabled the HSF to purchase buildings, hold them for a buyer willing to restore them, sell them to the buyer and use the proceeds to go again into the $200,000 fund. If losses were incurred, donors would replace the money needed to keep the Revolving Redevelopment Fund available for other purchases.

3. The completion of a professional inventory of Savannah's old buildings. "They studied approximately two thousand buildings in downtown Savannah, and of these eleven hundred were recognized as having architectural and/or historic significance." The goal was to produce a brochure to give Savannah's citizenry an idea of the value and significance of the older buildings within the town. "Over 1,100 buildings of architectural importance are now in the expanded *historic downtown.*"

4. The inauguration of a study of Savannah's tourism potential. This study included presenting the estimated value of preservation to Savannah's business and city government. By 1960 there were almost no private residences within the Historic District. At that time Savannah tourism was resulting in less than $100,000 a year, and the town had no bureau of tourism. Even the Chamber of Commerce was closed on the week-ends.

5. Focusing, on restoring an entire neighborhood, instead of the restoration of one house or building. One of the first areas to be targeted was the decaying West Side, the Pulaski-Jones

Street Project. According to Anna, "Historic Savannah had bought or taken option on 23 houses and sold 17 of them. Latest reports show 51 building units stabilized (restored or in process) and 39 reclaimed by Historic Savannah. . . ." By restoring blocks instead of single dwellings, HSF guaranteed that a person who invested in such an area would have neighbors who were also involved in restoration and keeping up the neighborhood.

6. To make full use of consultants from Charleston, Williamsburg and other areas of restoration, and to search out and apply to any national government projects (such as HUD), which might provide low-interest loans and other means of financial assistance for restoration.

7. Not only to get individual donors, but to get the backing of companies and organizations. For example, the Junior League was an early and significant donor ($25,000), and the Savannah daily newspaper (Anna's employer) not only provided financial backing, but also free advertising by way of significant articles favoring preservation.

8. The creation and/or expansion of walking tours, garden visits, bus tours, horse-drawn carriage tours, boat rides, and the establishment of the celebration and festivals of Georgia Day (February 12th).

Chapter 11

Anna Colquitt Hunter, Artist

It is hard to imagine just how busy Anna Hunter was in 1955. Her duties as a newspaper reporter had increased significantly. She not only reviewed books and reported on the comings and goings of Savannah society, she was also responsible for reviewing every artistic event that came to Savannah – art shows, theater productions, music, lectures – all came under Anna's domain. She also occasionally wrote editorials. In addition, she had inaugurated the HSF, which must have taken hundreds of hours of her time. It was almost as if she had taken on two full-time jobs. But that is not all. By 1955 she held a third "full-time" job: becoming a significant artist.

Before 1946 Anna's artistic endeavors existed mostly of small sketches and cartoons in her letters to friends and family. Although her *alma mater,* Agnes Scott College did offer classes in art when she was a student, her transcripts reveal that she never took any art classes or participated in either painting or drawing while in college. Her credits and her

interests at ASC were in writing, singing, and theater arts –
along with sports and social clubs.

Another indication that Anna was oblivious to her talent
in art can be found by looking at her sister Harriet Ross

Colquitt's cookbook, written in 1933. *The Savannah Cook
Book* is of particular interest for two reasons.

First, it has Savannah recipes that come primarily from
Savannah's blacks, who at that time were the cooks in most

households and restaurants. It also has many descriptions of black life and traditions at the time. Some are quite amusing. For example, Harriet asks a wonderful black cook:

> "How long do you cook your okra?" I asked a colored cook, to which she replied that she put it on when she did the rice. Knowing that the rice should cook about twenty minutes before steaming, I thought I would find out by this devious method, so I inquired "How long do you steam your rice?" "'Till dinner's ready," responded the wizard of the kitchen, and left me where I was when I started.

Second, the cookbook has simple drawings of blacks at work and a beautiful cover of a black cook being trailed by a hungry black cat. Anna Hunter could easily have done the artwork for her sister. But Florence Olmstead did instead. It is possible that Harriet Colquitt did not ask her sister to illustrate her cookbook because she didn't know Anna had artistic talent. Even more likely is that in 1933 Anna did not know herself about her artistic talents.

Anna gives a plausible reason as to why she began to participate in art when she was middle aged. "I took up painting in 1946 because as art critic of the *Savannah Morning News*, I found I could not write an intelligent review of exhibitions; and thought perhaps if I actually painted, I could judge better what the artist was trying to do. I have been trying to do it myself ever since."

Her statement makes sense – as far as it goes. But it overlooks Anna's deep, rich, colorful experiences in Oran and in Naples during the War. The areas where she was stationed in Africa and Italy could not have been more exotic and vibrant – and the people more diverse. In addition, her Red Cross job required Anna to study the design and decoration of

Recessional, 1949-1950
(Courtesy of Telfair Museums)

buildings – and to implement both into her facilities, no matter how temporary. These exotic places may have helped to awaken her slumbering talents.

Anna's involvement in the building and decorating of recreational facilities for R & R for soldiers provided her with a wonderful and unique background in art. Two of her initial paintings were of Africa and its people – done from memory.

Back in Savannah she joined a children's art class to learn the rudiments and techniques of painting. And obviously, she enriched her job as a newspaper art critic by taking up painting. In the *Savannah Morning News,* December 26th, 1946, she wrote an article entitled, "Why Don't You Paint?" In it she states:

All over Savannah and everywhere, are grown up people who have a secret urge to paint, and because they are adult and have never taken art (classes), they go on squelching that instinct to put something on canvas. They regard artists as persons born that way, and if the truth be known, as a little peculiar. Normal ordinary people just don't up and paint, they contend. Now something is happening and artists are cropping up out of the office, the kitchen and from behind the bridge table … (and) they are having an experience that is shaking them out of their old preconceptions, their ruts and inhibitions . . . . So let down your hair, boys and girls, and get out the brushes, for the sky's the limit in the art world today and one of you may be a Picasso or a Grandma Moses and never know until you try.

She took her own advice, often making vibrant paintings of the people and locales she knew so well: her beloved Savannah, various points of interest, flowers, and blacks, mostly doing simple jobs, such as hawking their wares. She also used her vivid imagination to depict various Negro Spirituals, with excellent results. One northern woman, who had purchased the painting *Joshua fit de Battle of Jericho* wrote Anna a letter. "She told of putting the newly acquired painting over her mantelpiece with trepidation for fear her Negro maid would take offense at the portrayal. Later she was relieved and thrilled to hear this person singing lustily the words of the spiritual."

Like everything else she was involved in, her drive and determination also revealed itself in her paintings. As her daughter recounts:

> [S]he was painting a water lily and wanted the real thing for a model. There was a water lily pond on the road which she passed every day. On a visit, she inveigled her daughter to stop and help her get a sample. As you may know, water lily roots go down to the center of the earth. Not at all deterred, Anna lay down full length on the bank, got her daughter to hold fast to her 70 year old legs, and reached for the water lily, triumphantly hauling it up and all 10 feet of roots after quite a struggle.

Her wonderful sense of humor often shined through her art. "The artist's whimsical sense of humor is quite apparent . . . . (Her) evident facility for creating a mood . . . cannot fail to affect even the most casual observer."

Even in old age, her wit did not desert her. Three examples of her sense of humor and her willingness even to become the butt of the joke and laugh at herself follow:

1. Long time companions tell of her strolling down Bull Street one day in a fancy hat which she thought very elegant, only to have a man come up and inquire what the hat said. Puzzled, she took it off to discover a note from her sister, "Anna, don't wear this hat without dusting it."

2. Once while in New York she decided to stop in for a service while passing St. Patrick's Cathedral. After tying on a scarf and entering quietly, she saw that the ushers had assembled at the front of the aisle to take up the collection. Hunter was uncertain that she had enough time to sit through this procedure, so she tapped the shoulder of an elegantly-dressed matron in front of her, and asked the time. The woman turned around looking slightly annoyed and handed her a dime.

3. One of the best oft told stories about Anna concerns the Rev. Bland Tucker of Christ Episcopal Church. He and Anna had sustained a mutual admiration society for some years and one morning he decided to take two visiting ladies to see the now-famous artist in her studio. The night before, Anna had had a party and the next morning discovered that she had thrown out some silverware with the trash. She went down to River Street to retrieve it and in addition to the silverware, she found a drunk who had spent the night in the dumpster. At that very moment, Rev. Tucker and the two ladies were on the bridge approaching Anna's front door. The good Reverend glanced down and saw Anna half into the

dumpster, where she was being embraced by the drunk. Quickly shepherding the bewildered guests back to his car, he said, sweetly, "I don't think this is the best day to call on Mrs. Hunter. We'll come back at a more propitious time."

Her art was an immediate success, coinciding with several artistic movements in America that stressed more realism and simple locales, such as the Ashcan School. Lamar Dodd, then the most recognized artist of Georgia, praised and encouraged Hunter's work, as did other artists and critics.

Two New York artists, Alexander Brook and Gina Knee, lived part time in Savannah, using as their residence and studio part of another cotton warehouse not far from Anna.

The three became friends. Both Brook and his wife Knee gave Anna particular encouragement in her art. They also let her use their New York apartment when they were away. One night when Anna was in their apartment, the next-door neighbors threw a particularly loud and boisterous party and woke her up. She called the police, who were slow in coming. Not happy with the continuous noise and music, she got up and knocked on the next-door neighbors' door. "When the police arrived, they found Anna dancing around in the arms of several of the [spirited] party goers!"

She showed her works in various cities primarily in the South and received much attention and acclaim. In addition she gave a one-woman show in New York City in 1948. The *Christian Science Monitor* wrote a positive review, concluding: "Living itself is grist to the mill of this delightful woman and much that is colorful and genuine finds itself caught in the fine mesh of her artistic genius."

The last art show she gave during her lifetime was a large retrospective given in 1973 at Savannah's Telfair Academy of Arts and Sciences. It was a huge success. Regarding her art objectives, Anna said, "I am interested in making the paint convey what is back of the representational – the humor, pathos, drama in everyday experiences or sights."

Her art reflected her philosophy, often creating ordinary scenes with extraordinary insight.

From Seaboard Docks, date unknown
(Courtesy of Telfair Museums)

Chapter 12

Anna Getting Older

At the age of sixty-six, Anna Colquitt Hunter retired from her job as a newspaper reporter, book reviewer, art critic, and editor on October 1st, 1958. She had kept her job for forty-five years. The *Savannah Morning News* later said, "She had gained prominence as an artist, and recognition as a leader in Savannah's historic preservation, but she would always be a newspaperwoman, first and foremost." To many in the Savannah newspaper business she would always be "our Anna." The newspaper article continues, "To say that she was a good newspaperwoman would be an understatement, indeed, excellent and superior are more fitting adjectives. . . . In retrospect, Mrs. Hunter's varied career seems something into which she was providentially led. It was only because her sister, the late 'Miss Hattie' Colquitt, was society editor of the old *Savannah Press* that she moved into the newspaper business, first as a substitute [even before her marriage] and then, finding it to her liking, full-time."

Many of her co-workers commented on how determined she was to get her story and to get it ready for print. The newspaper account of how Anna became a reporter is true. Her daughter Harriot became a psychiatrist as an adult and describes her mother's temperament in "Portrait of Anna," in *Anna's Annals.* Apparently, along with Anna's many wonderful traits, most of which typified the model Southern woman, she harbored three traits that only her family, other church and theater singers, and the men she dated saw: competitiveness, possessiveness, and jealousy.

Although Anna dearly loved her elder sister Hattie, "she strove to emulate her in very competitive ways."

Her jealousy was never more evident than when Harriot [Anna's daughter] first named her daughter after Hattie [Anna's sister] and then compounded the insult by naming her second daughter Julia Anne. We have mentioned her jealousy of George's sister, Julia and this brought it to the fore. "Anne" was chosen for Anna, which was a nickname some people had used for her but she did not appreciate the "Julia" coming first!

As has been seen, Anna was jealous if her husband even looked at another woman. After his death, her jealousy lingered to include the men who squired her around the town and took her to parties. Although she did not seem to desire marriage with any of them, she was instantly jealous if her date was late, especially if his tardiness included a tennis game for example that took too long – with a beautiful, or even a not-so-beautiful woman.

In earlier years she could sometimes even be jealous of her husband's "favoritism towards his daughters and resented, sometimes openly, his attentions to them." She could be competitive with her older daughter's intellectualism, although she often tried to hide it. She was proud of Harriot's accomplishments, but wished that she would "…be more feminine, like herself, to dress softly, in pretty clothes, to wear make-up and have boyfriends. Her younger daughter fulfilled these ambitions."

In spite of all of Anna's accomplishments, there was one thing more that she wanted to do: write the great American novel. Among her papers were several notes, snippets, ideas that she one day hoped to develop. She had already published some short stories and poetry, but that was not enough. Anna sometimes even seemed to be jealous of Margaret Mitchell. When it came to writing, being a highly successful newspaperwoman didn't seem to count for Anna.

When Anna's husband George died, her sister Hattie rescued her, allowing her and her children to stay in Hattie's house in Bluffton until she had sufficiently recovered. Hattie also helped Anna financially during this period. When Anna was nearly seventy, she got the chance to repay her sister. When Hattie became seriously ill, Anna took care of her in her Bluffton home. At that time Anna purchased a jeep to commute on mostly unpaved, narrow roads from Bluffton to Savannah. On her way back to Bluffton an old jalopy pulled out at high speed from what is now Hilton Head Road, heading directly for Anna's jeep. Attempting to avoid the fast-moving car, Anna swerved into a ditch, where her jeep overturned. Had it not been for an alert witness, she might have spent hours there. Although Anna survived with only minor cuts and bruises, this incident became one of a series of accidents that happened in Anna's senior years. She had several falls and broken bones, requiring long stays in a nursing home. As her eyesight grew worse, her paintings became brighter, her figures more primitive. Most difficult of all, her mental capacities, especially her memory, began to diminish.

In 1978 First Lady Rosalynn Carter visited Savannah and lauded Historic Savannah's Landmark project. That same year Anna, then age 86, broke her hip. Until that time she had remained alert and active and had received many awards for her work with the Historic Savannah Foundation. She had also shown her artwork in several shows in the South and in New York, for which she received significant praise and attention.

By 1979 the Historic Savannah Foundation could be characterized as a huge success. No longer were antiquated but potentially beautiful homes slipping through bureaucratic cracks and falling to the wrecking ball. Tourists were coming to see the fabulous old houses and gardens of the Historic and Victorian districts, and tasteful restaurants and hotels were springing up all over Savannah to accommodate them. Each year the tourist industry grew as did the publicity this splendid town engendered. What else could anyone do to make Savannah even more attractive?

Although historic houses seldom faced the difficulty of being torn down prematurely, another problem became more pronounced. What does one do with old mostly commercial buildings, ones that have been abandoned in favor of newer and more modern structures? Savannah was full of such buildings: old department stores, outdated schools and churches, an old guard armory, warehouses, old hotels and restaurants, even an old jail. Most of these structures did not lend themselves easily to restored housing projects, and what could one possibly do with an old jail – besides tear it down?

By 1970 many beautiful buildings had already been lost. In addition to the City Market (torn down in 1954), the huge and stunning Beaux-Arts Union Train Station lost its battle with the wrecking ball in 1963, as did in 1966 the once most beautiful hotel in all of Savannah (some say in all of the South): the DeSoto Hotel. How could this wanton destruction of beautiful buildings be curtailed?

Two unlikely couples then entered the scene: Richard G. Rowan and his wife Paula Wallace, along with Wallace's parents May L. Poetter and Paul E. Poetter. At the time Paula Wallace was pregnant. They all shared the same magnificent dream: to establish an art school in Savannah. Yet not one of them had any practical experience as to how to go about it, or even more important, how to pay for it. The money they had to invest in such a project came entirely from the Poetters' retirement. They had only decided that Savannah might make a more likely place for their project than their home town Atlanta.

They began their work by looking for a suitable building in which to locate their fledgling art school. At the time they were not particularly interested in preservation. They were just looking for a suitable building that they could afford. However, all that their finances seemed to allow was one of the old buildings scattered about the town. Paula Wallace stated, "Richard and I had been looking for potential properties all fall – old schoolhouses, abandoned hospitals, a morgue, empty factory warehouses, vacant downtown department stores, a deserted power station. At the time, none of us could know that eventually all those properties would become part of what we would build there."

After looking at a casket factory they came upon a gargantuan castle-like building called the Savannah Volunteer Guards Armory, built in 1892, and described at the time as a "grand ruin." It was a huge tumbledown three-story building with no heat, no air, little plumbing, almost no electricity and oh yes, "...the roof and walls needed extensive work." The two couples liked it, worried that it might be too big, but enjoyed the care, complexity, and sometimes even the humor that the architect William Preston put into the building. Ignoring all the dust, broken windows, and layers of grease from a dining room, they ". . . spent a quarter of a million dollars on a building in a ghost town." Looking out over the city from her "new" old building, Wallace said, "Much was ruined, wrecked, boarded, gloriously beautiful and derelict." Then the four founders of this tiny art school with one giant building shed their would-be titles (such as president and dean) to become janitors and day laborers in the clean-up of this monstrous building.

By the time they were ready to open their doors in the fall of 1979, they had one clean, partially restored armory building, a few certified art teachers and seventy-one students. In addition, they now had a name for their little school: the Savannah College of Art and Design, henceforth called "SCAD."

Almost from the beginning SCAD saw the value of investing in old, often abandoned Savannah buildings. It did not even try to build new buildings, as had Armstrong Atlantic when its campus was located in downtown Savannah. Instead, SCAD sought old buildings, often abandoned, and either bought them at very low prices, or was given the old building with the understanding that it would be renovated. The city was happy to give SCAD the jail free of charge. And high-priced professional workmen were seldom used. The students themselves provided much of the labor, under the professional eyes of their teachers. Instead of money for work, they got degrees, in very special areas such as professional restoration. SCAD sought students that were also artists and then gave them the backgrounds needed for specialized employment.

Today SCAD is a university – private, nonprofit, and accredited – offering more than one hundred academic degree programs in more than forty-two majors. In particular, students could major in different parts of preservation, taking courses in historic paint analysis, historic building systems, preservation technology or preservation law and advocacy.

The student's laboratory was right outside their window: Savannah, and later other countries, too.

From only Savannah in 1979, SCAD locations now include Atlanta, Hong Kong, Lacoste, France, and almost anywhere else via SCAD's online eLearning. The medieval French town of Lacoste gave many of its ancient buildings to SCAD, who promised to restore and keep them up. Now Lacoste is the location of many of SCAD's study-abroad students. In addition, SCAD's enrollment has gone from seventy-one in 1979 to more than twelve thousand undergraduates and graduates from more than one hundred countries.

Growing even faster than its enrollment is SCAD's prestige. This university does not believe in graduating an artist with no real job skills for employment. Students can major in countless areas of artistic design from advertising to photography, film, television, cinema, and preservation design. SCAD students often live, attend classes and work in restored buildings. Plus the university has state-of-the-art professional technology for its students as well as wonderful opportunities for collaborative projects with corporations, professional certifications, and internships. It almost goes without saying that a student from SCAD is well qualified. In fact, in 2014 the Red Dot Design Rankings placed this university among the top ten universities in Europe and America.

SCAD got its sprawling downtown campus by repurposing old Savannah buildings. How many downtown buildings have been touched by SCAD? Unbelievably, nearly sixty. And the Historic Savannah Foundation was responsible for the preservation and restoration of more than 370 mostly homes. Almost invariably, those who supported the Historic Savannah Foundation also supported SCAD. The old jail is now Habersham Hall, a late Victorian revival building with Oriental and Middle Eastern designs. Quite a beauty! A huge bank became a wonderful, luxurious gallery. Or consider the old Slater property. When SCAD acquired it, there was a huge hole in the roof, years of standing water and the threat of collapse. Now it grandly houses a bookstore, a gallery, an art supply store and a coffee shop.

Thanks to some foresight and a lot of sheer luck the goals and ideals of SCAD and the Historic Savannah Foundation weaved together, making both stronger. Each encouraged a new, old Savannah, as students, faculty, townspeople, and tourists began to fill up the once empty and abandoned spaces in the middle of their town.

Anna was too infirm to lend her full support to SCAD. Yet even in nursing homes her sense of humor did not fail her. She found a "new, old boy friend, a gentleman of ninety who naturally took a fancy to her." When members of the family asked the home for an update, a nurse informed them, "She's just fine. I believe she thinks she is running the place." Her daughter reported, "One day when I visited after an absence of some months, I leaned over to her in her wheel chair and said, "'Do you know me?'"

Anna Hunter Receiving the Oglethorpe Award

"She answered, 'Well, your face is familiar!' and laughed." When she did return to her apartment for about two years, with constant nursing care, she became more herself. But her clearer mind lasted only for a little while. As her daughter says of her, "She had courage and determination but simply could not function as she once did." On January 28th, 1985 Anna Colquitt Hunter died in a Tybee Island nursing home. She was ninety-three.

During her long lifetime Anna became the first woman ever to win Savannah's highest civic award, the Oglethorpe Trophy for her work in the restoration of the heart of her town, and for the establishment of the Historic Savannah Foundation, to ensure the wellbeing of historic homes and buildings. In so doing she greatly curtailed the often senseless gyrations of the wrecking ball. She also won the Thomas Gignilliat Award for her contributions to the culture of the community. In art she also won prizes and praise for her many exhibitions, particularly throughout the South. Her first exhibition at the Telfair Academy of Arts and Sciences in 1973 won serious acclaim. She was called a "sophisticated primitive" who could evoke wit and mood in her works. Some of her paintings of life in the South for blacks and whites preserve in pictures the life and times which are no more.

As many of her friends and relatives have attested, she could be selfish and possessive. As she herself has written, she could fly into a rage over a careless driver or the loss of a parking space. As her family noted, once in a posh restaurant she ordered chicken – all white meat – and burst into tears when the waiter gave her chicken – all dark meat. She could be jealous – of a singer in the church choir who might have gotten "too much" praise – of a suitor late for his date with her – of an actress who got the lead she wanted – of a beautiful woman her husband might have looked at. She might even have been jealous of Margaret Mitchel for writing such a great book. Although she tried to hide it, she could even be a little jealous of the love or praise her children sometimes got.

But when big things came along – raising a family without a father – relieving countless battle-worn soldiers from thoughts of war (if only for a little while) – saving a town from the thoughtless slaughter of its squares, homes, churches, businesses and schools – these acts she excelled at. One has only to walk along the beauty of the buildings and streets, birds and gardens that represent Historic Savannah today as in the past to recognize what Anna did.

Throughout most of her long and distinguished life Anna could superficially seem like an often "flirty" Southern Belle. Yet a closer look reveals profound differences. The old acronym LORD, used to describe the ideal Southern Bell, just did not fit Anna. Although she was loyal, the first letter in the acronym, she was not particularly obedient – not to anyone. As for respect, in the way it was initially meant, she often did not respect tradition, institutions or her elders. Nor did she gain respect for many of her actions and decisions. And her concept of duty was wildly different from its initial meaning. For Anna it was not her duty to go along with accepted mores and thought. It was not her duty to get married and spend the rest of her life serving the needs and desires of her husband. Married or not, Anna had no intention of being the "power behind the throne." Instead she believed that it was her duty to give back – to make significant contributions not just to her family, but to society and especially her community. Not only did she give back to her community in amazing ways, she stressed the importance of giving back to her children, her grandchildren and to anyone who would listen.

According to accepted thought, the chief duty of a true Southern Belle was to have a husband. In Anna's ninety-three years on earth, she spent seventy of them single. Clearly, she had several opportunities to re-marry following George's death. But she chose not to. Nor did she choose to live with a relative, as did so many other widows or spinsters of the time. At a time when it was so difficult for a woman to earn her own living, or even get a job, Anna not only supported herself, but in the first few years of widowhood she supported her three children as well.

As many have said, Anna was elegant without having money. She had style without flaunting it. She knew how to work, and even the biggest job did not cause her to hesitate. Not only could she convince, she could lead. No matter what the circumstances, she never forgot how to laugh – even at herself. Her work, her leadership, her intelligence, camaraderie and sheer energy ultimately transformed a sleepy little Georgia town with a once lovely, then rotting, center into one of the most attractive towns in the nation. Without her initiative in the 1950s, it is doubtful that SCAD in the 1970s would ever have seen the promise that lay within those abandoned, deteriorating buildings. The Historic Savannah Foundation that she founded could by 1979 (SCAD's first year) provide many before and after pictures of the promise and power of preservation. Anna Colquitt Hunter accomplished what others could or would not do. She saved a town.

Appendix A

More Information about the Six Ladies Who Helped Anna Found the Historic Savannah Foundation

1. **Katharine Judkins Clark** had always enjoyed the beauty and even the quirks of old homes. She and her husband, Reuben Grove Clark moved to Savannah in 1948. They lived in an older home on Gaston Street in what would become the Historic District. Later they lived in the 1793 Odingsell House on East St. Julian Street, the oldest house in Savannah. Kass, as nearly everyone called her, began her preservation work in earnest when she became the chairman of the committee in charge of the restoration of the Owens-Thomas House after it was bequeathed to the Telfair Academy, where she later became a trustee.

This house was one of the finest examples of Regency architecture in the nation. "She cajoled wealthy donors, architects and craftsmen to save the building, which is now a museum operated by the Telfair Academy of Arts and Sciences." If the little group dedicated to the preservation of Savannah's Historic District needed anything, it was someone who excelled at "cajoling" wealthy Savannahians and other possible donors. As a plus, her husband was also a banker.

Kass served the American Red Cross working as a nurse's aide in Walter Reed Hospital during World War I and again in Albany (New York) Hospital during World War II. She was instrumental in getting an American Red Cross chapter established in Savannah. And she helped to found the tour of homes, which benefited Savannah's Christ Church and St. Luke's Church on Hilton Head Island.

2. **Jane Adair Wright** was the only person in the preservation group who was never married. She resided with her father, the Reverend David Cady Wright, who was rector of Christ Episcopal Church. Like all of the other women of this group, Jane was active in most civic affairs. She also helped to found the Junior League of Savannah. In addition, she was executive secretary of the Chatham-Savannah Tuberculosis Association and was a member of the Georgia Historical Society and the Trustees Garden Club. She also served as interim director of the Girl Scouts.

Her interest in the historic district resulted in her becoming the chair of Savannah's first Tour of Homes and Gardens, held in 1955. "We charged $1 for our first tour," Miss Wright said.

"Altogether, we made $50 that day – and were absolutely delighted and proud of ourselves."

3. **Lucy Barrow McIntire** was the oldest member of the group at age sixty-seven in 1953, and like Anna, was a widow. Born in Athens, Georgia in 1886, the daughter of Judge Pope Barrow, once a governor of Georgia and then a senator, Lucy McIntire was greatly respected by nearly

everyone in town – and not just because of her ancestry. "Miss Lucy" as nearly everyone called her was more than just a little interested in Savannah – its problems as well as its progress.

In 1909 she married attorney Francis Percival McIntire; they had six children. However, her large family did not seem to slow Lucy down regarding her community affairs. In earlier times, she helped to found two national organizations in Savannah: the League of Women Voters and the Junior League of Savannah. She served as first president of the latter. She was also president of the Savannah Suffrage Association and the Georgia Federation of Women's Clubs. Her ardent support of Woodrow Wilson resulted in her appointment as the first Georgia Committeewoman on the Democratic National Committee.

In the 1930's Miss Lucy received an appointment as Field Supervisor for Roosevelt's Works Progress Administration (WPA). Part of that work included anthropological studies of the Indians and their mounds in central and eastern Georgia. During World War II she founded the Soldiers Social Service of Savannah (USO) and also became Service Director in Savannah for the American Red Cross. Few people in all of Georgia were better connected both politically and in the field of social services than Miss Lucy.

She helped to establish the free lunch program in the Chatham County schools years before federal government involvement. "She was also a founder of the Savannah Nursery School, the Women's Relief Committee, the Juvenile

Protection Association, the Savannah Health Center, the Chatham Nursing Home, and Savannah's Christmas Stocking, in addition to serving as president or on the boards of the Bethesda-Savannah Children's Center, Child Placement Services, Social Services Exchange, the Crittendon Home, United Community Services, and the Council of Social Agencies of Savannah-Chatham County. In addition to her volunteer efforts Mrs. McIntire held several professional positions." She knew everyone in town, most of the important people in the state, and some even in Washington, including the late Franklin D. Roosevelt.

She also appreciated the arts. She wrote poetry and helped to found the Georgia Poetry Society, where she won several prizes during her forty-four year membership. And just like Anna, she participated in community theater. She authored one prize-winning production which was presented in New York City in 1928. Theater, writing, art, and the Red Cross: both Anna and Lucy shared these interests.

Lucy Barrow McIntire remained active in Savannah events throughout her long life. When the Civil Rights Movement swept into Savannah in the 1960s and even earlier, Lucy Barrow McIntire led the move toward integration and helped to smooth white acceptance of this movement in Savannah. "In her seventies she spoke out in favor of civil rights for African Americans with the same enthusiasm with which she had supported women's suffrage half a century earlier."

4. **Elinor Louise Adler**, then age 50, was one of the younger members of the group. Along with her husband Sam G. Adler, she did a great deal of work both with and for Savannah's Mickve Israel Synagogue. She was also on the Women's Board of Bethesda, the Family Service Board, and took part in Savannah's Little Theater. In addition, she was a member of the Record Club and the League of Women Voters. Sam Adler and his family had held ownership in the Savannah Dry Goods Company, one of the most important department stores in Savannah, for over 100 years.

Her husband's business contacts and standing in Savannah were enormous. He also served on the board of the Savannah Bank and Trust Company; he contributed to many philanthropic endeavors and helped to found the Savannah Symphony Orchestra.

Sam Adler also served in both World Wars. In World War I he served in the Army overseas as a first lieutenant in the 82nd Division – 319 Field Artillery – from 1917 to 1919, for which he received the Silver Star. In 1943 he re-entered the service, this time commissioned as captain. He remained in service for the next five years, advancing in rank to lieutenant colonel. In 1946 he served as Assistant State Director of Selective Service. From 1947-1948, he served in Berlin with the General Staff Corps, Office of the Military Government of the United States. He authored two military books: *All this for Georgia Veterans,* and *German Manpower in World War I.* He received the Army Commendation Medal for his service in World War II.

Although it was his wife who first took interest in the improvement of Historic Savannah, Sam Adler would also become one of the most important people in Savannah regarding preservation and what would later become the Historic Savannah Foundation.

5. **Nola McEvoy Roos** was a noted civic, business, and political leader in Savannah. She was the public relations director of Civil Defense and also became the first female Clerk of Council in 1949, thereby becoming the first woman to hold any top-level job within the City of Savannah. She also served as vice-president of the Chatham-Savannah Board of Education and as vice chairman of the Chatham County Democratic Executive committee. In 1938 she was elected president of the Chatham County Democratic Women's Club. In 1940 she served as district census director – at that time becoming only one of four women within the United States to have that position. She was particularly interested in the Business and Professional Women's Club, where she served as local and state president.

She was also fund-raising chairman for the American Red Cross, and board member of the Girl Scouts Council, as well as chair of the recruiting committee for the Woman's Army Auxiliary Corps (WAAC) in World War II. In addition, she was a board member of the Girl Scout Council, and a member of the Better Business Bureau. Along with her husband, Louis J. Roos, who was prominent in both state and local Jewish originations, she owned and operated Roos

Qualité Pecan Company and Georgia Paper-shell Pecans and Pecan Meats.

6. Dorothy Ripley Roebling was the wealthiest woman of the group. Her husband's great grandfather, John Roebling, and his grandfather, Col. Washington Roebling were in charge of building the Brooklyn Bridge. "Their success stemmed from the wire cable business John founded." In the 1950's Dorothy's husband managed that company. "The firm's contracts included the George Washington and the Golden Gate Bridges."

Dorothy (her friends and husband called her "Dickie") became aware of the damage that so-called "progress" was doing to beautiful old homes and buildings many years before her move to Savannah. As she put it:

> Having grown up in a small New Jersey city full of beautiful old homes which surrounded small parks, rather like your squares and equally steeped in historic interest, then later living in a similar nearby town both of which, at the close of World War I, experienced the terrible pressure of the population explosion, the motor-car and the dream of progress at any cost, I was aware of that same restless bull-dozer bearing down on the beautiful pattern and continuity of ancient Savannah. Serenity, superb architecture and irreplaceable workmanship were apparent here thirty years ago but elsewhere, fast disappearing in one city after another and there seemed to be no chance or even interest in attempts to halt the avalanche.

"Dickie" belonged to many of the same organizations as the other members of the group: the Junior League, the

Trustees Garden Club, and the Art Association, – but then she veered off the normal path by becoming a member of the Savannah Association of Retarded Children.

The story of Dorothy, her husband Robert C. Roebling and their fabulous 170-foot three-masted schooner, the *Black Douglas* would make a great adventure novel. Built in 1930 by the Bath Iron Works the schooner served in peace and war (particularly World War II); was used as a research vessel for scientific study by the United States Fish and Wildlife Service, sailing routes from Alaska to southern California; has served as a school, and also became a ship for treasure hunters, particularly in the Caribbean. The vessel was then reconditioned in Lemwerder, Germany, "...serving as a template for super yachts." The *Black Douglas* is unique primarily because of her steel hull, which most scholars claim was the largest ever built. The *Black Douglas* has also been named *te Quest, Aquarius, Aquarius W.* and presently *El Boughaz I,* now owned by King Mohammed VI of Morocco. The ship has fared well, once owned by one of the richest men in Georgia, and presently owned by one of the richest men in the world.

However, there was a dark side to the wealth of Robert and "Dickie." Shortly after their marriage in 1925, Robert and "Dickie" designed and built "Landfall," a 10,000-foot stone mansion (still in existence) at 8 Landfall Lane in Princeton, New Jersey, which was completed in 1928. With the stock market crash of 1929 the Great Depression began in the United States. Then on December 5, 1932, the United States ratified the Eighteenth Amendment ending Prohibition. The rum-runners and other gangsters associated with huge liquor profits then found themselves out of a job. They began to look for new sources of easy money. One popular consideration of these miscreants was kidnapping the children of the rich and holding them for huge ransoms. After all, in March of 1932 the kidnapping of Charles Lindbergh III, then age twenty months, served as a great example and led to the payment of a $70,000 ransom, in spite of the fact that the baby was later found murdered. The kidnapper simply set a ladder up against the second-floor window of the nursery, climbed up, entered, and snatched the baby. What money-making scheme could be easier than that? In 1932 the Lindberghs lived in Hopewell, New Jersey, not far from the Roeblings' mansion.

As Carol Megathlin states, "Because of its notoriety, one tends to think of the Lindbergh kidnapping . . . as unique, but actually such acts were widespread." The Roeblings had five children. Not long after the Lindbergh incident the Roeblings' governess surprised an intruder climbing up through the window of the Roebling nursery. The kidnapping was foiled only by the chance entrance of the governess.

Following the attempted kidnapping, the Roeblings put their eighteen-acre Princeton estate, called "Landfall" up for sale and moved into the *Black Douglas* where there could be no possible entrances through windows. They sailed around South America. After that voyage, a friend invited Bob to visit a hunting preserve called Modena Plantation on Skidaway

Island off the coast of Georgia. At the time this island was only accessible by boat.

The Roeblings loved the Modena Plantation, particularly since its harbor was deep enough to hold the *Black Douglas,* and purchased it. For some time the Roebling family still lived on their ship, moored at the dock of the Modena Plantation. By the time "Dickie" accepted Anna's request to become one of the Seven Ladies, the Roeblings had turned Modena Plantation into a large working farm, where their family resided for many years. In fact, in the 1940 U.S. census, Robert Roebling listed his profession as "farmer." In 1967 Robert Roebling donated his herd of Aberdeen Angus cattle to the state in return for a marine research center on the island. That donation resulted in the internationally famous UGA Institute of Oceanography, which has flourished on Skidaway ever since.

**Portrait of Dorothy Roebling
1934 by William Paxton**

Seated: Lucy Barrow McIntire, Elinor Adler Dillard, Anna Colquitt Hunter

Standing: Nola McEvoy Roos, Jane Adair Wright, Katherine Judkins Clark

Appendix B

Samples of Anna's Art

Nearly all of the samples of Anna Colquitt Hunter's art in this section come from photographs owned by her family. Unlike museum-quality work, these are often flawed (the picture is crooked, the lighting is poor, there is a flash reflection, etc.). Yet until an art professional prepares a true identification, classification, and analysis of Hunter's art, these photographs remain the best way to get an idea of Anna's work. Looking at these photographs of Anna's art does reveal her creative gifts and inspirations. At present these photos are the best representation of the art of this artist and are meant to be enjoyed rather than scrutinized.

In the few cases where they are known, we have included the title of her works.

Ice Cream Man

Shellin' Beans, *by Anna C. Hunter*

Skaters, *by Anna C. Hunter*

Skaters, probably the first version

Another Time, Another Place

Church of the Cross

Oyster Roast

Waterfront

Gull Rondo

Acknowledgments

I could not possibly have written *Restoring Lost Times* as it is without the help of Anna Colquitt Hunter's descendants. In particular, Dr. Harriet Ross Jardine coordinated the family in providing not just information about her "should-be" famous grandmother, but also gave me photos of much of her artwork. George Jardine's, Julie Jardine's and Nancy Hood's contributions to pictures and artwork were also invaluable. For this book most of the original sources came directly from this family. I cannot thank them enough for their time, interest, and wonderful resources.

Dr. Edward Michael Staman created both the design of this book and its technical aspects. I cannot thank him enough for his patience and skill. Karen Staman, professional editor and ghost writer for research physicians, provided significant corrections and thoughtful suggestions for making Anna's story tighter and to the point.

Marianne Bradley, Library Administrative Coordinator/Archives Manager of the McCain Library at Agnes Scott College enabled me to take a look at Anna Hunter as a young woman first attending college. Ms. Bradley's considerable resources and research helped me immensely. The staff at the Bull Street Library of the Savannah Live Oaks Public Library was very helpful, particularly the librarians in the Local History Room. Mr. Daniel G. Carey of the Historic Savannah Foundation was also cooperative, as was Ms. Jamie Credle, Director of the Davenport House.

Composer-in-residence at the 2017 Savannah VOICE Festival and creator of the opera *Anna Hunter, The Spirit of Savannah,* Michael Ching, provided significant comments and suggestions as we exchanged e-mails from the summer of 2016 until November 2017. Working on the same subject, but each in a different venue proved challenging and exhilarating.

Thanks also go to Lesley Francis and Kristyn Fielding for helping me to get the word out. Other acknowledgements go to the Georgia Historical Society, Mr. and Mrs. Edie Culver (for introducing Anna's art to me), Shirley Oelshig for her knowledge of the times, Linda Porter for her pointers about Savannah, and the editorial suggestions and corrections of Dr. Edwin Chase, and Dr. Anne Jones. I would also like to thank Laura Staman and Fran Eckert for their constant support and encouragement.

NOTES

CHAPTER 1

SAVANNAH'S FIRST ESCAPE

11. "dreadful to look upon.": Davis, *Sherman's March,* 6.
11. "the flames seemingly nothing.": Trudeau, *Southern Storm,* 87.
11. "mercy in his composition.": *Ibid.*
11. "every friend on the road.": Davis, *Sherman's March,* 29.
13. *"Arnold, Mayor of Savannah.":* Trudeau, *Southern Storm,* 497.
14. "thousand bales of cotton.": *Ibid.,* 508.

CHAPTER 2

ANNA'S ANCESTORS AND EARLY CHILDHOOD

15. "that trip was a mistake.": Jardine, *Anna's Annals,* 3.
16. "Colony of Georgia.": Jardine, "Biological Summary" *Anna's Annals,* 1.
17. "the grief I feel.": King, *EbbTide,* 118.
17. "they were not divided," Jardine, *Anna's Annals,* 4.
19. "classics by the hour," Jardine, *Anna's Annals,* 3.
20. "we were free agents.": *Ibid.*
20. "hilarity, laughter and teasing.": *Ibid.*
22. "more than just pretty.": *Ibid.*

22.   "when Anna was twenty-four.":
       http://www.loc.gov/pictures/item/csas200800671/.
       Accessed 8/25/2017.
22.   "(180 days in Georgia.":
       http://www.georgiaencyclopedia.org/articles/education
       /public-education-prek-12. Accessed 7/29/2017.
23.   "Anna Columbus in School.": Jardine, *Anna's Annals,*
       4.
26.   "Randolph-Macon and Wellesley.": Hall, ed. *Service
       through Knowledge and Character,* 36-37.
26.   "occurred within their family.": Hall, ed. *Service
       through Knowledge and Chacter,* 54.
27.   "same to you, Miss Pape!": Hall, ed. *Service through
       Knowledge and Character,* 32.
27.   "rivet your attention.": *Ibid.*
27.   "illness at the time": *Anna's Annals,* 5.

CHAPTER 3

MARRIAGE

32.   "choir was well known.": Jardine, *Anna's Annals,* 6.
32.   "apparently picked it up.": *Ibid.*
32.   "her forget it.": *Ibid.*
34.   "the family dearly.": *Anna's Annals,* 7.
34.   "of child abuse.": *Ibid.*
34.   "and threatening fantasies. : *Ibid.*
34.   "she hated her mother.": *Ibid.*
36.   "had a sly sense of humor.": *Anna's Annals,* 5.
36.   "hugging and kissing.": *Anna's Annals,* 5-6.
36.   "happen to her.": *Anna's Annals,* 6.
37.   "decline in sight.": Bartley, *The Creation of Modern
       Georgia,* 169.
38.   "home to go to.": *Anna's Annals*, 10.
38.   "continuous dry sobs.": *Anna's Annals,* 10.
39.   "Don't be silly.": *Ibid.*
40.   "driving me crazy.": *Ibid*
40.   "Carolina Chickadee.": *Ibid.*
40.   "take care of her.*"*: *Anna's Annals,* 10-11.
40   "loved that work.": *Anna's Annals,* 11.

40   "ought to double it.": *Ibid.*
41.   "Who is Franco?": "Portrait of Anna" in *Anna's Annals,* 3.

CHAPTER 4

THE WINDS OF WAR

45.   "faith in our tradition.": Poem located in the index of *Anna's Annals.*
46.   "lose its luster.": Anna's small handwritten journal, 12/17/43.
46.   "identification papers.": Anna's small journal 12/9/42.
46.   "in my mind.": small journal, 1/10/43
48.   "keep up work.": small journal, 12/16/42.
48.   "Charleston or somewhere.": small journal, 2/15/43
48.   "hideous missions.": small journal, 4/12/43.
48.   "by its sound.": small journal, 1/9/43.
49.   "war is too far away.": small journal, 1/1/43.
49.   "recruiting here. Boys.": small journal, 1/6/43.
49.   "reconstruction work later.": small journal, 12/8/42.
50.   "age of 51.": *Anna's Annals,* "Biographical Summary," 1.

CHAPTER 5

THE RED CROSS

51.   "being in the Army.": small journal, 7/23/43.
51.   "patients – so young.": small journal, 7/21/43.
51.   "in human nature.": small journal, 8/5/43.
53.   " step on Him!": small journal, 7/23/43.
53.   "I believe I is.": small journal, 10/1/43.
53.   "I want to go!!": small journal, 10/2/43.
54.   "worlds to conquer.": small journal, 10/3/43.
54.   "start training tomorrow.": small journal,10/5/43.
54.   "the hounds did.": small journal, 10/31/43
54.   "on two Frenchmen.": small journal, 10/12/43.
55.   "before his eyes.": small journal, 10/21/43.

55.   "had poisonality.": small journal, 10/22/43.
55.   "he screamed.": small journal, 10/26/43.
55.   "French restaurant in N.Y.": small journal, 10/27/43.
55.   "when we will go.": small journal, 10/22/43.

CHAPTER 6

ANNA IN AFRICA

57.   "like Biblical pictures.": large journal, 11/28/43.
57.   "over open fire.": large journal, *Ibid.*
57.   "scenery is beautiful.": large journal, *Ibid.*
58.   "what I can do.": large journal, 12/2/43.
61.   "I am thrilled.": large journal, 12/10/43.
61.   "necessity and self-preservation.": Bell, *France and Britain 1940-1994,* 19-20.
62.   "historic rivals, the British.": Purnell, *Clementine,* 260.
64.   "view which is beautiful.": large journal, 12/11/43.
64.   "like a throne.": large journal, 12/11/43.
65.   "children in rags.": large journal, 12/16/43.
65.   "carols, and fudge.": large journal, 12/24/43.
66.   "cactus on rocks in front.": large journal, 1/22/44.
66.   "cheese on toothpicks.": large journal, 2/22/44.
66.   "is the real thing.": large journal, 2/26/44.
68.   "ever have felt so.": large journal, 1/6/43.
69.   "so close to war.": large journal, 2/26/44.
69.   "pain in back continue.": large journal, Late Feb./44
69.   "daughters in the States. *Anna's Annals,* "Portrait," 3.
70.   "there is a reckoning.": large journal, 11/19/43.
70.   "largely to these.": large journal, 11/19/43.
70.   "go into it all . . .": large journal, 11/20/43.

CHAPTER 7

ANNA IN NAPLES

71.   "get there if not now.": large journal, 5/24/44.
71.   "try for India later.": large journal, 5.28/44.
72.   "called it the Belfry!": large journal, 6/11.

72.   "and the mountains.": large journal, 8/8/44.
72.   "up in air)" large journal, 8/22/44.
72.   "miss my club sorely.": *Ibid.*
73.   "very characteristic.": large journal, 8/24/44.
73.   "[see this view].": large journal, 8/25/44.
73.   "interesting features.": large journal, 8/26/44.
73.   "mass of soldiers.": large journal 8/27/44.
73.   "miserably detached.": large journal 9/4/44.
73.   "tried to walk.": large journal, 9/8/44.
74.   "kitchen not complete.": large journal, 9/25.
75.   "I enjoy them tho.": *Ibid.*
75.   "did not always co-operate," large journal, 10/2/44.
76.   "Mrs. Hunter and her aides . . .": *Anna's Annals,* 15.
77.   "war in this theatre.": Inglesby, "To Whom Honor is Due," *Savannah Magazine*, September, 1947, p. 25.
78.   "facilities each month.": *Anna's Annals,* 18.

CHAPTER 8

ANNA'S RETURN TO SAVANNAH

84   "her column finished.": "To Whom Honor is Due,": *Savannah Magazine,* September, 1947, 25.
86.   *"with a dirty face.":* Russell & Hines, *Savannah,* 175.
86   "ravaged by smallpox.": Ibid.
86.   *"to destroy itself.":* Russell & Hines, *Savamnah,* 176.
87.   "we see today.": Brannen,"Proudly presenting our Heroines," VII.
89.   "and cultural facilities.": Adler, *Savannah Renaissance,* 3.
89.   "be demolished later.": *Savannah,* 178.

CHAPTER 9

FOUNDING THE HISTORIC SAVANNAH FOUNDATION

91.   "In haphazared fashion.": Cooper & Lawton. *Savannah's Preservation Story,* 2. For an excellent summary of the various people who also contributed to the preservation of the Historic District, this book is very good.

92.   "50-foot roof line.": *Ibid.*

93.   "no sanitation at all.": Telephone interview with Freeman Jelks, Jr. by Jamie Credle, February 14, 2005.

94.   "could be found for it.": Anna's speech on the establishment of the Historic Savannah Foundation. 2-3.

95.   "bunch of radishes.": *Savannah's Preservation Story,* 7.

95.   "an irreplaceable loss.": Adler, *Savannah Rennaisance,* 8.

95.   "in the ciy's eye.": Russell and Hines, *Savannah,* 179.

96.   "Kass, Jane, and myself.": Anna's speech on the establishment of the Historic Savannah Foundation, 3.

97.   "and business world.": "Lucy McIntire, Georgia Women of Achievement.

98.   "unimaginable in the 1950s.": Courtesy of the Bureau of Tourism.

98.   "6. Tourism.": Anna's Speech, p. 7.

98.   "in the 1950s.": These figures come from "Visit Savannah".

98.   "graduated from college.": https://www.statista.com/statistics/184272/educational-attainment-of-college-diploma-or-higher-by-gender/. Accessed 6/28/2017.

99.   "high school in 1940.": https://nces.ed.gov/pubs93/93442.pdf 77. Accessed 6/28/2017.

100.   "grew Historic Savannah.": Emory Jarrot, Telephone interview with Jamie Credle.

100.   "I might say gunpowder.": Anna's speech on formation of Historic Savannah Foundation, 3.

101.   "were being lost.": *Savannah: A History of her People.*
       176.

CHAPTER 10

GROWTH OF THE HISTORIC SAVANNAH
FOUNDATION

105.   "partitions all around.": Freeman Jelks, Telephone
       interview with Jamie Credle.
105.   "with the ladies.": *Ibid.*
105.   "bad for business.": *Ibid.*
107.   "the group's headquarters.": *Savannah,* 180.
107.   "according to longtime friends.": Minis, "Artist's
       Portrait," *Georgia Gazette* 2/12/79, 26.
108.   "telling me what my job was.": Minis, *Ibid.*
108.   "original city plan.": Anna's speech, 7.
108.   "early April Flowers" *Adler,* 6.
110.   "and professional execution.": Anna's speech, 1.
110.   "who would restore them.": Adler, *Savannah
       Renaissance,*, 91.
111   "more time to take action.": *Ibid.* 13.
111.   "and courageous undertakings.": Anna's speech, 7.
111.   "a one-man movement.": *Ibid.* 19.
111.   "plus a bank – that counts.": Anna's speech, 7.
111.   "proud of ourselves.": HSF file, "50 Years of Southern
       Charm."
112.   "wealth, be recaptured.": "Savannah's Preservation
       Store," *Savannah Morning News,* 1960 in Hunter file
       of Live Oaks Library.
112.   "at a crucial hour.": Anna's speech, 9.
113.   "in the expanded *historic downdown.": Savannah,*
       185.
114.   "by Historic Savannah. . . .": Anna's speech, 10.

CHAPTER 11

ANNA COLQUITT HUNTER, ARTIST

117.   "when I started,": *Savannah Cook Book.* xvi.
117.   "myself ever since.": *Anna's Annals* "bio..": 23.
117.   "never know until you try.": *Anna's Annals,* 22.
91.   "words of the spiritual.": *Anna's Annals,* 24.
120.   "after quite a struggle.": *Anna's Annals,* "Profile," 3.
120.   "most casual observer.": *News and Chronical,* Charleston, Oct. 1950.
120.   "without dusting it.": *GA Gazette,* "Artist's Portrait," 27.
120.   "handed her a dime.": *Ibid.,* 28.
121.   " more propitious time.": *Anna's Annals,* "Portrait of Anna," 5.
122.   " party goers!": *Ibid,* 8.
122.   "of her artistic genius.": *Anna's Annals,* 23.
122.   "experiences or sights.*": Ibid.*

CHAPTER 12

ANNA GETTING OLDER

125.   "her liking, full-time.": *Savannah Morning News,* 3/31/1985, front page.
125.   "competitive ways.": *Anna's Annals,* "Portrait of Anna," 7.
125.   "'Julia' coming first!": *Ibid.,* 1.
126.   "not-so-beautiful woman.": *Ibid.*
127.   "his attentions to them.": *Ibid.*
127.   "fulfilled these ambitions.": *Ibid.*
128.   "spent hours there.": *Ibid.,* 3.
130.   "would build there.": Wallace, *The Bee and the Acorn,* 33.
130.   "as a 'grand ruin.'": Wallace, 7.
130.   "needed extensive work.": *Ibid.,* 7-8.
130.   "building in a ghost town.": Ibid., 39.
130.   "beautiful and derelict.": Ibid., 41.

133. "a fancy to her.": *Anna's Annals*, "Portrait of Anna," 6.
133. "running the place.": *Ibid.*
135. " and laughed.": *Ibid.*
135. "as she once did.": *Ibid.*

APPENDIX A

More information about the Six Ladies Who Helped Anna to Found The Historic Savannah Foundation

135. "won serious acclaim.": *New York Times,* May 1, 1993.
140. "proud of ourselves.": "The Tour: 50 Years of Southern Charm." in HSF files, 3/24/85.
142. "several professional positions.": "Lucy Barrow McIntire," Georgia Women of Achievement.
142. "a century earlier.'" "On the 50th Anniversary of HSF." in HSF files.
145. "business John founded.": Megathlin, Carol. "Modena Plantation," http://www.skio.uga.edu. Accessed 6/10/2017.
145. "Golden Gate Bridges.": Carol Megathlin, "About the Roeblings.": *Ibid.*
145. "halt the avalanche.": "Moderna Plantation" *Ibid.*
146. "for super yachts.": Megathlin, *Ibid.*
147. "acts were widespread. *Ibid.*

Bibliography

Unpublished Works

Clark, Reuben Grove III. Eulogy: Katherine Lee Judkins Clark, April 1993. "A Life of Great Personal Constancy and Achievement."

Hunter, Anna Colquitt. "Anna Colquitt Hunter Papers." Georgia Historical Society.

Hunter, Anna. small journal, Begins December 7, 1942.

Hunter, Anna. large journal, 1943-1944.

Hunter, Anna. "Historic Savannah, Incorporated: Its Beginnings, Its Goals, and Its Accomplishments, 1955-1960." Speech by Mrs. Anna Hunter, to the Friends of the Library, February 13, 1968.

Jardine, Harriot Hunter. *Anna's Annals: Anna Colquitt Hunter,* 1892-1985.

Publications

Adler, Emma. "A Dedication to a Dedicated Savannahian." *Historic Savannah.* Vol. 8, No. 2, March/April, 1985.

Adler, Lee and Emma Adler. *Savannah Renaissance.* Charleston, SC: Wyrick & Company, 2003.

Adler, Leopold (Lee) II. Obituary. *Savannah Morning News.* 1/31 to 2/1/2012.

Agnes Scott College, *Silhouette* Yearbook, 1910-1911

Agnes Scott College, *Silhouette* Yearbook, 1911-1912

"Anna C. Hunter." "Our Opinion," *Savannah Evening Press.*"
     1985

"Anna Colquitt Hunter." *Savannah Morning News.* 1/31/1985.

"Anna Hunter suggests a Project for H.S.F. *Historic Savannah
     Newsletter.* 5/21/76.

Bartley, Numan V. *The Creation of Modern Georgia.* Athens,
     GA: The University of Georgia Press, 1983.

Bell, Malcolm Jr. *Historic Savannah.* Savannah: Historic
     Savannah Foundation, n/d.

Bell, P.M.H. *France and Britain 1940-1994: The Long
     Separation.* Routeledge, Taylor & Francis 1997.

Blair, Ellen Simmons. Obituary. *Savannah Morning News.*
     9/14/2005.

Bynum, Russ. "Lee Adler, Historic Preservationist, Dies at
     88." Associated Press, 1/31, 2012.

Carey, Daniel G. "Girl Talk Womanly Wisdom Saves the Day
     (and Our Cities)." *Skinnie.* Vol. 13, issue 8, 4/12/2015, p.
     13.

Clark, Katherine Lee "Kass" Judkins. Find a Grave Memorial.

Clark, Reuben Grove. Ancestry.Com

Coffey, Tom. "Anna Hunter, Preservationist, Artist, Dies at
     91." *Savannah Morning News*, 1/29/85, Obituary.

Coffey, Tom. Lorraine Johnson-Coleman, Bret Lott, Margaret
     W. DeBolt. *Seasons of Savannah.* Ronald P. Beers,
     Community Communations, Inc. 200.

Coffey, Tom. "Anna C. Hunter Is Dead at Age 91." *Savannah
     Morning News,* p. 1A, 1/30/85.

Colquitt, Harriet Ross. *The Savannah Cook Book A Collection
     of Old Fashioned Receipts from Colonial Kitchens.*
     Charlston Walker, Evans & Cogswell, Co., 1933.

Cooper, Polly Wylly and Laura Connerat Lawton. *Savannah's
     Preservation Story. 2016.*

Davis, Burke. *Sherman's March.* New York Random House, 1980.

"A Dedication to a Dedicated Savannahian." *Historic Savannah.* Historic Savannah Foundation, vol 8, no 2, March/April, 1985.

Dick, Susan E. and Mandi D. Johnson. *Savannah 1733 to 2000.* Charlston, SC: Arcadia Publishing, 2001.

Dillard, Elinor Adler. Obituary. Fifty Years Ago. *Savannah Morning News*, 8/6/1992.

"Factors Walk Shopping." *Savannah Scene.* September-October, 2016, 48.

Hall, Patricia J., editor. *Service through Knowledge and Character.* Brentwood, TN: The Savannah County Day School, 2005.

Hunter, Anna C. "Alas, The Truth Is Being Told About the Ladies." "Woman's World." *Savannah Morning News,* 2/24/1958.

Hunter, Anna C. "Horns, Tails and 5 Brains." "Woman's World," *Savannah Morning News.* 12/31/1957.

Hunter, Anna C. "Letters from Old Friends." "Woman's World," *Savannah Morning News.* 1/12/1958.

Hunter, Anna C. "The Merry, Merry Yuletide." "Woman's World." *Savannah Morning News.*12/15/1957.

Hunter, Anna C. "New York Christmas Worth Chair Car Ride." "Woman's World." *Savannah Morning News.* 12/24/1957.

Hunter, Anna C. "A Trip Up The Beautiful Ogeechee River." "Woman's World." *Savannah Morning News.* 1/5/1958.

Hunter Anna C. "A Woman Behind the Wheel." "Woman's World," *Savannah Morning News.* Library on Bull Street files.

Inglesby, Edith. "To Whom Honor is Due," *Savannah Magazine,* Sept., 1947, 25.

Jaynew, L. C. Brigadier General, USA. Hunter Commendation to Red Cross Delegate, Stirling Tomkins. 18 December 1944, Georgia Historical Society.

"Katherine J. Clark, 95, Georgia Preservationist. Obituary. *New York Times*. May 1, 1993.

King, Jr., Spencer Bidwell. *Ebb Tide As Seen Through the Diary of Josephine Clay Habersham, 1863.* Athens, GA University of Georgia Press, 1958.

Lawton, Laura C. *Legendary Locals of Savannah.* Charleston: Arcadia Publishing, 2015.

Lebos, Janet Leigh, editor. *Savannah: A Southern Journey.* Savannah Area Tourism Leadership Council, *2011.*

Lewis, Wendi L., ed. *Seasons of Savannah.* Montgomery, AL: Community Communications, Inc. 2000.

McIntire, Francis P. Chatham County GA Archives, biography.

McIntire, Lucy Barrow. *Find a Grave Memorial.*

McIntire, Lucy Barrow. Georgia Women of Achievement. Inducted 1997.

McIntire, Luby Barrow. On the 50th Anniversary of HSF. "From 'Miss Lucy." 7 Ladies File, HSF.

McNair, Walter Edward. *Lest We Forget An Account of Agnes Scott College.* Atlanta, GA.: Tucker-Castleberry Printing, Inc., 1983.

Minis, Margaret. "Artist's Portrait," *The Georgia Gazette and Journal Record,* Feb 12, 1979 p. 26.

Mobley, Chuck. "X Marks the spot The Desoto Hotel." *The Skinnie.* Vol 15, Issue 9, 10-15.

Obituaries for Nov. 27, 2002 "James William McIntire." In Bull Street Library file.

Obituary in HSF files. "Dorothy Ripley Roebling: April 4, 1904-May 21, 1977."

Obituary in HSF files. "Mrs. Nola Roos, Civic Leader, Dies in Atlanta," December 24, 1980.

Obituary in HSF files. "Jane Wright Is Dead at 90." 3/3/91.

"Our Opinion Anna C. Hunter." *Savannah Evening Press,* in files of the library on Bull Street.

"Our Savannah 2014-2015," *Savannah Morning News,* in files of the Live Oak Library on Bull Sreet.

Pinkerton, Connie Caposola, Maureen Burke, Ph.D., and the Historic Preservation Department of the Savannah College of Art and Design. *The Savannah College of Art and Design Restoration of an Architectural Heritage.* Charleston, SC: Arcadia Publishing, 2004.

Poetry Society of Georgia. Records. Georgia Historical Society.

Purnell, Sonia. *Clementine The Life of Mrs. Winston Churchill.* New York: Viking, 2015.

Russell, Preston and Barbara Hines. *Savannah: A History of her People since 1733.* Savannah Frederic C. Beil, 1992.

Savannah Evening Press, "A Life of Great Personal Constancy and Achievement:' Katherine Lee Judkins Clark – April, 1993," Obituary, April, 1993.

Savannah Evening Press, "Historic Preservationist Elinor Adler Dillard Dies," obituary, 8/6/92.

"Saving Ourselves Savannah's Preservation Movement, True History in the Making." Our Savannah 2014-2015 *Savannah Morning News,* p. 41.

Sewell, Cliff. "Noblesse Oblige 'Miss Lucy' Knows the Meaning" *Savannah Morning News,"* found in the Bull Street Library's file on the Seven Ladies.

Sparks, Andrew. "They're Fighting to Save Old Savannah" in Anna Hunter file in the Bull Street Library, Savannah.

Spracher, Luciana M. *Lost Savannah Photographs from the Collection of the Georgia Historical Society.* Charleston, SC: Arcadia Publishing, 2002.

St. Arnaud, Charles. *Bonaventure Cemetery Savannah, GA.:* Savannah, GA Charles St. Arnaud.

Stramm, Polly Powers. *Sentimental Savannah Reflections on a Southern City's Past.* Charleston, SC: The History Press, 2006.

"The Tour 50 Years of Southern Charm." In HSF files, March 24, 1985.

Trudeau, Noah Andre. *Southern Storm: Sherman's March to the Sea.* New York Harper Collins Publishers, 2008.

Varnedoe, Catherine [granddaughter of Lucy Barrow McIntire]. "A Woman Named Catherine. *Savammah Morning News.* 4/19/2015.

Wallace, Paula Susan. *The Bee and the Acorn.* New York: Assouline, 2016.

Wittish, Rich and Betty Darby. *The Insiders' Guide to Savannah.* Falcon Publishing, Inc., 1999.

Works Progress Administration (work by Lucy McIntire). District 8 Scrapbook and Photo Album.

Wright, Jane. "Jane Wright is Dead at 90" Obituary, March 3, 1991.

Online Articles

"A 30-year History of Savannah College of Art and Design." http://savannahnow.com/julia-c-muller/2009-02-21/30-year-history-savannah-college-art-and-design. Accessed 1/15/2017.

Ancestry.com. "1940 United States Federal Census." Accessed 2/15/2017.

"Dodd, Lamar (1909-1996)." www.georgiaeneyelopedia.org/articles/arts-culture/lamar-dodd-1909-1996. Accessed 6/20/2016.

"History of Historic Preservation." *New Georgia Encyclopedia.* http://www.georgiaencyclopedia.org/articles/arts-culture/history-historic-preservation. Accessed 5/16/2017.

Holland, Marcus. "150 Years of the Savannah Morning News, 1850-2000. People. "Hunter's Contributions Go Beyond

Newspaper. http://savannahnow.com/features/150years/PEOhunter.shtml. Accessed 4/25/2017.

Hunter, Anna Colquitt. GA Women of Achievement. Inducted in 1995. http://georgiawomen.org/2010/10/hunter-amma-colquitt/. Accessed 6/16/2017.

Megathlin, Carol. "Modena Plantation," http://www.skio.uga.edu. Accessed 4/30/2017.

"Our Museum—Davenport House" http://www.davenporthousemuseum.org/our-history. Accessed 8/25/2017.

Roebling, Dorothy Ripley. "Modena Plantation." Signed by D. R. Roebling, www.skio.peachnet.edu/aboutus/history/roebling/roeblin-_family.php. Accessed 5/22/2017.

Roos Obituary "Mrs. Nola Roos, Civic leader, Dies in Atlanta," Obituary, 12/24, 1980," http://www.davenporthousemuseum.org/wp-content/uploads/2010/09/NolaRoos.pdf

"Nola Roos Obituary," 1980, Ancestry.com. Accessed 3/15/2017.

"Schooner, Black Douglas," *Wikipedia*. Accessed 5/1/2017.

United States Federal Census, 1940. Ancestry.com. Accessed 5/15/2017.

Interviews

Adler, Emma. With Clare Ellis and Cornelia Groves, notes by Jamie Credle, January 3, 2002.

Butler, Betty. Interview by John Dickinson, Coastal Oral History Project, 2/13/2007.

Carey, Daniel. Phone Interview with Author, summer, 2017.

Chisholm, Frank and Katherine, interviewed by John Dickinson, Coastal Oral History Project for the Davenport House Oral History Project, 2/15/07.

Cooper, Emmeline. "Conversations with a Friend: Emmeline Cooper's Slices of life." *HSF's 50th Anniversary.*

Cooper, Emmeline King. Information by Cooper given to the HSF, telephone interview, 10/21/05, by Jamie Credle, now in HSF's file.

Credle, Jamie. Interviewed by author, summer, 2017.

Ellis, Clare and Cornelia Groves, interview by Jamie Credle, 6/14/05.

Jardine, Hetty. Several telephone and in-person interviews with Dr. Jardine from May, 2016 through November 2017.

Jelks, Freeman. Telephone interview by Jamie Credle, February 14, 2005

St. Arnaud, Charles. *Bonaventure Cemetery Savannah, GA.* Savannah, GA Charles St. Arnaud.

Index

n.b.: City of Savannah and Anna Hunter appear on almost every page.

L

M

N

O

P

R

About the Author

A. Louise Staman has won many awards for poetry, biography, and one children's story. Her first biography was about the murder of a famous publisher in Paris: *With the Stroke of a Pen,* published in both French and English. Staman has won three national awards, one state award and a plaque from the Georgia Commission on Women for her second biography, *Loosening Corsets.*

Restoring Lost Times is Staman's third biography. She has discovered that the topic of women in Georgia's history has largely been ignored. Yet their stories are often fascinating and their triumphs significant.

She presently resides in Savannah with her husband of over fifty years. They have three daughters and three grandchildren.